M000102782

Business Wisdom
of the
Electronic Elite

Enjoy !

Geoffrey James

Business Wisdom
of the
Electronic Elite

*34 Winning Management Strategies
From CEOs at Microsoft,
COMPAQ, Sun, Hewlett-Packard,
and Other Top Companies*

GEOFFREY JAMES

TIMES BUSINESS

RANDOM HOUSE

Copyright © 1996 by Geoffrey James

All rights reserved under International Pan-American Copyright Conventions. Published in the United States by Times Books, a division of Random House, Inc., New York, and simultaneously in Canada by Random House of Canada Limited, Toronto.

James, Geoffrey
    Business wisdom of the electronic elite / Geoffrey James.
        p.   cm.
    Includes bibliographical references and index.
    ISBN 0-8129-6379-2
    1. High technology industries—Management.   2. Corporate culture.
3. Organizational effectiveness.   4. Office practice—Automation.
5. Leadership.   I. Title.
HD62.37.J349   1996
620′.0068—dc20   96-3559

Random House website address: http://www.randomhouse.com/

Printed in the United States of America on acid-free paper

9   8   7   6   5   4   3   2

First Edition

For Anthony J. Robbins,
who taught me to live my life
with passion and courage.

Acknowledgments

This book would never have happened if I hadn't been surrounded by people who have supported me throughout the creative process. These people include (but aren't limited to):

My parents—all four of them—who have always encouraged me to be the best that I can be. Their support is behind everything I do, and I'm deeply grateful that I've been blessed with so much love in my life. I'd also like to thank my sisters and brother for continuing to believe in me and what I am trying to create.

Jonathan Seybold, who recognized qualities in me that I didn't know I possessed, and who has always been willing to give me advice on my career and on the development of my ideas.

Gerald Rafferty, whose wisdom and perceptiveness has been a guiding beacon in my life for the past nine years, and who remains my dearest mentor and friend.

Eric Nee, who took time from his busy schedule to tutor me on how to get interviews from the Electronic Elite and how to make the most of the time I spent with them.

Sunnie Reardon, who offered help and advice, especially when it looked as if things weren't coming along as quickly as I had hoped.

My friends from YMAA, especially Tracey Majkut, Jeff Pratt, Ramel Rones, and Jim O'Leary. It's great to know that I have friends I can count on through the thick and thin of life. This especially includes Master Yang Jwing-Ming, whose instruction, care, dedication, and affection are vastly appreciated not only by myself but by everyone who knows him.

My special friends: Marc Kalish, Melissa Bernhardt, Jody Carlson, David Foote, Jack Mandelbaum, Ann Palermo, Scott McReady, Martin Heller, and Tom Austin, all of whom reviewed my ideas in the early phases of the project and offered valuable comments.

My former editor Teri Hudson, who worked with me to develop the concept and tried her best to get it into publication sooner.

The publicity people for the Electronic Elite: Steven Timm, Jill Shanks, Kevin O'Connor, Jessica Kersey, Emory Epperson, Richard Eckel, Susanne Vagadori, Patty Dalheim, Jennifer Heller, Jennifer Rothert Piercey, Cecile Roux, and Joni Mialovich, among others.

The people who have attended my seminars and presentations over the years and the clients who have hired me to coach them in new areas of business development. I have learned more from you than you have learned from me.

The wonderful people of Hollis, New Hampshire (my new home town), the folks at Tokyo Japanese Steak House and Sushi Bar in Nashua, and Nancy Falco, my truly excellent transcriptionist.

My literary agent Claudette Moore, who's done a lot of hand-holding as we moved this project through its various stages.

My editor at Random House, Tracy Smith, whose intelligent and perceptive criticism has made this a far better book than it otherwise would have been.

And especially the Electronic Elite. I appreciate that these extraordinarily busy and important people took the time to help me with this project and to review my work. I hope that they'll consider this to be their book as much as it is mine.

GEOFFREY JAMES
GeoffJames@aol.com
New Hampshire, 1996

Contents

Introduction

Fifteen years ago, the most sophisticated piece of technology on the average worker's desk was a telephone, a device that's been around for a hundred years. Today, nearly everybody in the typical office copes with personal computers (PCs), fax machines, voice mail, cellular telephones, networks, electronic mail, mobile computing, the Internet, and all the paraphernalia of modern computer technology. That this vast influx of technology has changed the business world is an understatement. Work everywhere has become more hectic, more frenzied, as information and ideas fly around the "wired" corporation with the speed of light.

The purpose of this book is to prepare you, and your organization, for the brave new world that technology has brought us. It does this by sharing the hard-won experience of a new generation of business leaders, the very people responsible for the technological revolution that is changing every aspect of our working lives. These management pioneers—I call them the "Electronic Elite"—are responsible for the growth and continuing success of some of the most dynamic corporations in today's business world.

These corporations include software giant Microsoft, the number one PC manufacturer COMPAQ, and rapidly expanding Hewlett-Packard. They also include lesser-known companies such as Silicon Graphics, which sells high-powered workstations, or Intuit, whose Quicken software package turned personal finance into the latest computer craze, or Dell Computer, which grew in 10 years from a dorm room hobby into a multibillion-dollar corporation.

The characteristic these diverse companies share is that they've all grown and expanded in the face of massive competition. To thrive in today's computer industry, organizations must become both flexible and powerful, able to pursue long-range goals yet nimble enough to change directions at a moment's notice. If your industry is becoming more competitive and your company must cope, then you may find it valuable to learn how the Electronic Elite have consistently succeeded in the world's most highly automated industry.

According to the Electronic Elite, the key to long-lasting success in fast-paced industries is to create a new kind of corporate culture. And, indeed, when you look at the companies of the Electronic Elite, you discover that they aren't at all like the industrial giants of yesteryear. To most people, the world of "big business" means conservatism, wool suits, power lunches, and executives who order about low-paid corporate "troops." That scenario may have worked before computers, but today things just aren't the same.

The Electronic Elite are different from the business leaders of the past. They exhibit little of the posturing, paranoia, and obsessive controlling behavior that characterizes many Industrial Age executives. Here's what I mean:

TRADITIONAL EXECUTIVES SAY	ELECTRONIC ELITE EXECUTIVES SAY
Bigger is better, biggest is best.	Stay lean, run hard, move quick.
Markets are territory to be conquered.	Treat customers like business partners.
Destroy the competition and leave no wounded.	Compete today and cooperate tomorrow.
Hide your mistakes from the other sharks.	Let the organization learn from your mistakes.
Lecture employees on company loyalty.	Throw a company party in the parking lot.
Install a computer so you can cut headcount.	Let people buy the computers they need.
Always keep the bastards guessing.	Always explain why you've made a decision.
You can't trust people, especially employees.	Let people alone and they'll do the right thing.
Success is having a big staff and a big budget.	Success is feeling good about what you do.

The Electronic Elite are living examples that not only is success in the information age compatible with enlightened business practices—it is dependent on them. The cynical old rules of the traditional corporation have simply become obsolete.

The corporate cultures of Electronic Elite companies are built on respect for the individual. Employees are encouraged to make their own decisions; personal excellence and dedicated teamwork are commonplace; and people believe that employees should have a chance to become millionaires. It's a corporate culture that values informality, blurs the distinction between "work" and "fun," and considers productivity an outgrowth of integrity and mutual respect. In short, it's a very different corporate culture from that found in most of today's corporations.

This new corporate culture harnesses the power of computer technology. The "command and control" management techniques that worked in the precomputer era aren't effective when employees at every level can communicate worldwide in a matter of seconds. The only way to achieve true productivity is by using computer technology to unleash the latent creativity that the old-school big business mentality has always sought to repress.

This means changing the basic business beliefs that people hold about what it means to be a manager, what it means to be an employee, and what it means to conduct business. The Electronic Elite share core beliefs about business that are different from those of most corporate managers.

As you believe, so you behave. Executives who are deeply convinced that employees are childlike troops who should only follow orders will inevitably create rigid, controlling, hierarchical organizations. On the other hand, executives who believe their employees are intelligent adults who can be trusted to do the right thing create organizations that are relaxed, flat, and nimble. Because today's technology-driven workplace favors the flexible organization, managers who want to remain effective must assimilate and disseminate core beliefs that support this flexibility.

This book is your opportunity to learn the core beliefs of the most successful leaders in the high-tech business world. The first seven chapters will guide you through this internal transformation. Through case studies, exercises, and relevant quotations from the Electronic Elite themselves, you'll slough off obsolete business beliefs and replace them with more relevant attitudes.

This book also includes a method for helping your organization to evolve a flexible, elite culture. Chapters 8 through 11 provide a road map for extending new influences inside the corporation.

Throughout the book are numerous quotes from some of the most successful of the Electronic Elite. These quotes, edited slightly for clarity's sake, offer you the opportunity to learn directly from the best and the brightest in the high tech business world.

Starting with Chapter 2, each chapter introduces specific management strategies, 34 in all, that the Electronic Elite use to make their organizations powerful and flexible. These strategies are completely congruent with the new corporate culture and they work because that new culture provides an intellectual and emotional framework to support them. However, I have a word of warning: If you're not willing to adopt the mindset of the Electronic Elite, don't bother trying the 34 strategies. Without new beliefs, these techniques simply can't take root.

My challenge to you—should you choose to accept it—is to become a cultural revolutionary. Successful corporate cultures result from the thoughts, intentions, and energy of everybody in the organization. While managers naturally have a greater influence on the process, there are people inside every organization who set the tone for the way the organization works. Often these cultural leaders have more influence over the eventual success of the organization than the people officially tasked with "running" it. This book will help you become a catalyst for transforming and improving your workplace.

This book can do something else for you. Even if you feel that you don't have energy or influence to change your current organization, you can learn how to survive and thrive in the "wired" corporation. Your current company may be hopelessly obsolete but this book can guide you toward a brighter future inside a more evolved organization.

The business wisdom in this book can help any individual or organization weather the winds of technological change that are transforming the business world. Think about it! Wouldn't you like to experience, in your company, the same kind of excitement, the same kind of success, that the Electronic Elite have enjoyed?

If that sounds good to you, read on . . .

Business Wisdom
of the
Electronic Elite

Chapter One

Who Are the Electronic Elite?

I'd like you to meet some interesting people, who run (if that's the right word for it) the most exciting and successful companies in business today. Several of these companies you no doubt know about. Others might not be as familiar, even though they're part of an extraordinary revolution, not only in technology but in management as well. You need to know about the people who run these companies because they've written new rules for corporate success that really work in today's swift-moving markets. I call these people the *Electronic Elite*.

They're a diverse lot. Some, like Bill Gates (Chairman of Microsoft) and Mitchell Kertzman (CEO of the Powersoft database tools company) are college dropouts. Others, like Safi Qureshey (Chairman of AST Research, personal computer market leader in the Far East) and Eckhard Pfeiffer (CEO of COMPAQ, the largest manufacturer of personal computers), are from foreign countries. Still others, like Sally Narodick (CEO of Edmark, which builds educational software for children), come from traditional management backgrounds. Many of the Electronic Elite have had unusual religious experiences. Mitch Kapor, founder of Lotus (the 1-2-3 spreadsheet company) taught meditation. Apple cofounder

Steve Jobs is rumored to have entered business after an encounter with a guru in India. In general, these people are younger than the typical CEO. Michael Dell (founder of Dell Computers) is 30. Hewlett-Packard's Lew Platt at 54 is the eldest of the group.

Their diverse backgrounds, however, do not mean that these individuals have nothing in common. In fact, nothing could be further from the truth. What unites them is a new way of thinking about business that is very different from the conventional wisdom of the Industrial Age. When you listen carefully, you discover that these new leaders don't sound like typical dyed-in-the-wool-suit executives. They use different words, draw different parallels, apply different imagery. There's a restless dynamism about them that's hard to resist. They don't posture (at least not very much). They don't act paranoid when confronted with new ideas. They have a very different mindset than the executives of the past.

Unlike the "good ole boys" who run the traditional computer companies like IBM, Digital, or Unisys, this new generation of business leaders comprises highly creative entrepreneurs who've built the modern computer industry. The Electronic Elite bring a unique quality of leadership to the business world. They've created organizations that are wildly productive and yet humane in their treatment of employees. Their companies look different and feel different from the typical corporation. Bureaucracy is almost nonexistent. Janitors hobnob with vice presidents. There's an egalitarian energy that inspires employees to try to change the world. The Electronic Elite have discovered how to create organizations of astounding creativity and flexibility. They are true role models for the managers of the future, not just in the computer industry, but in other industries as well.

It's stating the obvious to point out that computers have changed the world. The effect of computers on nearly every aspect of our daily lives is so pervasive and so complete that it's difficult to envision the modern world without them. Our economic systems are completely dependent on computers to measure, transmit, and verify financial transactions. The global telecommunications network that brings information from around the world to our living rooms and boardrooms is a result of this vast technological explosion. Computers are everywhere, embedded inside our automobiles, televisions, and microwave ovens. The personal computer has become nearly as common as the telephone on the desks of American workers.

The computerization of the business world has had an enormous effect on corporations, and as a result many of the most respected corporations of the past are experiencing intense stress. Corporations are struggling, and in many cases failing, to meet the challenges of computer technology. Corporate downsizing has become so common that it doesn't even make the news most of the time. Middle managers, sacked in midcareer, wander through job searches like lost ghosts, hoping against hope that this is just a temporary setback. Wherever you look, the business news brings tidings of great change.

No industry has been harder hit than the computer industry itself, where a group of the most respected companies in the world—traditional computer vendors including IBM, Digital, and Wang—have stumbled and declined, only to be replaced as industry leaders by a group of relative upstarts—companies such as COMPAQ, Microsoft, and Intel. This wholesale transformation is amazing because the traditional computer vendors had all the cards stacked in their favor. They had money, they had experience, they had customers, they had fabulous technology. And yet, despite that leverage, they were not able to maintain either market position or profitability.

The decline of the traditional computer vendors and the rise of the Electronic Elite can serve as an object lesson for what's happening to businesses around the world. The once-respected giants of many industries are suffering (even as the traditional computer vendors suffered) from upstart competition arising in unexpected places. Managers and leaders in every industry need to cope with, and take advantage of, massive market change. What better role models than the Electronic Elite, who through a painful process of trial and error, have learned what works and what doesn't work in the business environment of the future?

I'll be telling you more—a lot more—about the Electronic Elite, the companies they lead, and the strategies they use to create winning organizations. You'll discover the secrets of their unparalleled success, and learn about a new kind of corporate culture. But before we look at these exciting innovations, we need to go back in time, so that we can understand the market conditions that gave rise to the Electronic Elite in the first place.

A LITTLE HISTORY

The 1970s were glory years for the computer industry, full of energy and optimism. The invention of the integrated circuit made it possible to create computers that were faster and more powerful than ever before. Demand for computers was high, and profit margins were even higher. Career advancement was automatic. Anyone lucky enough to be employed by a computer vendor was guaranteed a bright future.

The traditional computer vendors were dominated by IBM, which made more money each year than all its competitors combined. IBM's competition was a set of mainframe vendors that had been around as long as IBM itself. These were the so-called BUNCH, an acronym that stood for Boroughs, Univac, NCR, Control Data, and Honeywell. In addition to the BUNCH, a group of vendors sold the smaller mainframes called minicomputers; these vendors included Digital, Data General, Prime, Wang, and a host of others.

Until the early 1980s, it looked as though the computer industry's glory years would continue forever. Profits were up. The traditional mainframe and minicomputer vendors seemed to just keep on growing. Few people inside the computer industry guessed that in another five years or so, all of it would be a memory.

What changed the computer industry was the microprocessor. The microprocessor was a "computer on a chip" that made it vastly less expensive to provide computing power to individual workers. This radical drop in the price of computer power changed the way that computers were manufactured, distributed, purchased, and used. In the 1970s, computers were so big and so complicated that customers were forced to buy from a single vendor, who sold the entire unit as a big-ticket item. These transactions involved so much money and effort that the computer vendor and the customer needed a very close relationship. Some IBM salespeople, for example, even had their offices at their customer's establishment.

The microprocessor changed all this. The old minicomputers and mainframes were cumbersome, complex devices. The microprocessor, on the other hand, made it possible to put the power of a mainframe on everyone's desktop. Rapid advances in technology made computers so cheap that the computer power that would have cost $1,000,000 in 1970 had dropped to about $100 by 1995. To put this into perspective, if computers were automobiles, you could buy the transportation equivalent of a 1970 Toyota for about a dollar today.

The microprocessor also meant that computers could be sold off the shelf, like stereo systems. It was no longer necessary, or economical, to have high-priced salespeople at customer sites. For many applications, a customer could buy a computer at a local storefront computer store. Whereas in the past purchasing a computer had been a major corporate decision requiring the signature of everybody but God himself, now just about anybody could afford to buy a personal computer. Lowly line managers with microscopic budgets could afford as much computer power as the corporate heavies who ran the giant mainframes. This created an explosion of buying activity, as professionals around the world began to demand—and receive—control over their own computing resources.

The microprocessor also fueled an amazing burst of creativity in the field of software. Programmers began designing new products that could take advantage of this new source of inexpensive computing power. Excellent word processing, spreadsheet, and database programs flooded the market.

The microprocessor and the ensuing software revolution created an enormous demand for computer products. And where there's demand, there's money to be made. Somebody was going to reap the profits. Who better than the traditional computer companies who had been building and manufacturing similar products for almost 20 years?

Think about it! The traditional minicomputer and mainframe vendors had everything going for them. They had plenty of cash, more than enough to launch new methods of manufacturing and marketing. The traditional vendors also had great technology. After all, IBM actually invented the standard personal computer that's so popular today. Similarly, Digital, the minicomputer vendor, had software in the 1970s—such as electronic mail and electronic conferencing—that's only now becoming common on personal computers and networks. Even more important, the traditional vendors had reputations for being very well run. IBM, for example, was consistently listed in *Fortune* magazine as the most widely respected company in the world. Digital's founder Ken Olsen was, as late as 1988, being touted in the business press as the "ultimate entrepreneur." Big war chests, great technology, legendary management—a recipe for certain success, you'd think. But it didn't work out that way.

By 1995, the BUNCH had disappeared in a flurry of mergers and downsizings. Univac and Boroughs had merged and shrunk beyond recognition. Honeywell's computer division had emigrated to France, only staying alive as the result of government charity. NCR had vanished into AT&T only to reappear in a blaze of layoffs. Control Data had almost completely disappeared.

The minicomputer vendors fared little better. Wang declared bankruptcy. Prime and Data General shriveled into nonentities. Digital, once the darling of Wall Street, saw its stock plummet from a high of $199 to a shaky $28 while managing to lose $1.75 billion in a single quarter, an incredible amount considering that Digital's earnings peaked at $1.3 billion a year in 1988. Of the 10 or so minicomputer vendors that were profitable in 1980, only Hewlett-Packard remained a major force in the industry 15 years later, having successfully diversified into personal computer printers and engineering workstations.

Of the traditional mainframe vendors, only IBM is reasonably intact. However, it was recently forced to lay off nearly half of its 400,000-plus workforce merely to remain profitable. IBM has watched its lead in personal computers shrink year after year and has seen upstart competitors eat away at its market share. While IBM is financially stable at the time of this writing, it's unclear whether this can remain the case unless the company recaptures some of its lost industry leadership.

Despite the troubles of the traditional computer vendors, the computer industry as a whole has continued to grow. This growth, however, has been captured by an entirely new set of companies. Some of these upstarts are software companies such as Microsoft (operating systems), Wordperfect (word processing), Lotus (spreadsheets), Novell (networks), and Oracle (databases). Some, including COMPAQ and Dell, make personal computers; and others, like Sun and Silicon Graphics, make high-priced specialty workstation systems. While a number of the traditional computer vendors are still around in watered-down, stripped-to-the-bone incarnations, it's clear to people both inside and outside the computer industry that a "changing of the guard" has taken place.

The irony here is that according to conventional business wisdom, the large, established vendors should have had no problem making the transition to the new products. By all rights, they should easily have been able to overpower the upstarts such as Microsoft and Apple. An entire industry, consisting of some of the most respected companies in the world, was driven into obscurity and financial ruin by raggle-taggle upstarts seemingly coming from out of nowhere. Needless to say, this wholesale market transformation caught a lot of people by surprise—especially the employees of the traditional vendors, some half a million of whom found themselves pounding the pavement, looking for new jobs. And most of these people had just one question on their minds: "What the #%@! happened?"

Less surprised, but more pleased, were the people who founded the "upstarts" that stole industry leadership away from the traditional vendors. These companies—the companies of the Electronic Elite—have grown apace, creating wealth for founders, employees, and stockholders alike. However, the bare facts of the changing of the guard don't get at the essence of what's useful for us to know. What was it about these upstarts that allowed them to perform so well in the face of such powerful and entrenched competition? Since they didn't have more money, more brains, or more technology, what was their competitive advantage?

THE QUEST FOR THE SECRETS

For the past 10 years, I've been obsessed with finding the answers to those questions. This obsession is rooted in my personal experience. In my 20 or so years working in the computer industry, I've watched the great drama unfold. I've experienced some of the pain and dismay that resulted from the Humpty-Dumpty tumble of the traditional vendors. And I've also been privileged to work with the upstarts from the beginning of their rise to power and prestige. The contrast I saw between the old and new drove me to discover the secret of what it *really* takes to be successful inside these fiercely competitive markets.

It's been a long and difficult quest. I buried myself in the voluminous literature about management, reengineering, and corporate change. I coordinated million-dollar market research projects to discover the inner workings of the computer industry. I talked with hundreds of insiders, from chief information officers (CIOs) in corporate boardrooms to computer geniuses in advanced laboratories. I spoke at industry conferences and listened to what the other pundits had to say. Finally, I interviewed the Electronic Elite themselves, to discover, from their own perspective, the true secrets of their success.

One of the first things that struck me during my conversations with the Electronic Elite is that they feel that they're part of a different culture. They believe that they've made a radical departure from the management styles and corporate behaviors of the past. The first member of the Electronic Elite who clued me in on this was Mitchell Kertzman, the CEO of Powersoft, a company that makes database software for personal computers and networks.

Mitchell is a highly interesting person. As a young man, he made his living as a booking agent for rock 'n' roll bands, sold biorhythm charts through the mail, and even worked as a disc jockey for a while. Although he never completed college, Mitchell is a formidable business leader. Starting Powersoft as a one-man show, he grew the company until its recent sale to Sybase, another software company, for almost a billion dollars. I asked Mitchell why IBM had failed to maintain its position of leadership inside the computer industry. He told me that it was culture that made all the difference:

> IBM simply got too bureaucratic to be nimble when technology changed. Today, technology changes so rapidly that you need a flexible, agile, nimble culture and management. If your culture is bureaucratic, you will not succeed in technology—period. You won't catch the waves. It's like an ocean liner trying to surf. The waves aren't going to move you, you're not going to see the currents, you're not going to catch the waves. You have to be much lighter and much more agile. IBM had a strong culture, but it eventually worked against them when the market changed.

The Electronic Elite believe that their organizations are successful because they have successful cultures. Since the Electronic Elite think that culture is so important, we need to examine the concept more closely.

What kind of corporate culture leads to success? In the recent past, the most powerful and successful companies have been those that were centralized and autocratic, IBM, for one. By 1990 or so, all of that had changed. Relatively decentralized companies, including Microsoft and Hewlett-Packard, had overtaken their more centralized competitors. Something must have changed inside the business environment to make decentralized companies into more effective competitors than the centralized companies that preceded them.

What happened was the computerization of the workplace. In the 1970s, most computers were still being used for only specialized functions, such as accounting and engineering. While many companies had bought word processors, these were used more as sophisticated typewriters for secretaries than as productivity tools for managers and professionals. Personal computers were rare or nonexistent. As mentioned earlier, in 1980, the fanciest device on the typical manager's desk was the telephone, which had been around for over a hundred years!

By 1990, however, personal computers were everywhere. Most professionals now had immediate access to an almost unbelievable amount of computing power. New, easier-to-use word processing and spreadsheet programs had made computers accessible to the average employee, most of whom embraced the new technology like a long-lost friend. Not only that, many of these desktop computers were being hooked up to computer networks, allowing people to send electronic messages to one another at the speed of light. Not since the Industrial Revolution of the nineteenth century had there been such an explosion of new technology. And it all happened in the space of a decade.

During the Industrial Revolution, the "explosion" of technology took place over a period at least 10 times longer. Even then, the social changes that resulted were massive—a complete transformation of the ways people worked and lived. For example, in the rural, agrarian culture that preceded the Industrial Revolution, few people worked regular hours. Many workers made the bulk of their income as temporary help during harvest and planting. Other workers plied trades, such as weaving or blacksmithing, that allowed them to toil at their own speed. Workers were either tied to the land or extremely mobile, going wherever there was demand for their services.

This seasonal style of working, while appropriate for a primarily agricultural society, was inappropriate for the burgeoning factories of the Industrial Age. Factory workers had to be present during scheduled hours for a factory to function effectively. During the early years of the Industrial Revolution, factory owners were plagued by workers who continued to behave like farmhands.

Employees would come and go as they pleased, disappearing after payday and then reappearing after their money had run out. This was such a serious problem that legislatures actually enacted laws requiring regular factory attendance. Over time, the need for a prompt and reliable workforce created the modern industrialized city. The entire society had to adapt in the face of the new technologies.

Major changes in technology demand major changes in culture. In a global sense, culture, not technology, always has determined which nations have prospered. For example, few people realize it, but much of the technology of the Industrial Revolution was invented in China—gunpowder, movable type, accurate clocks, just to name a few. However, these innovations fell on the sterile ground of a highly traditional agrarian culture that was unable, or unwilling, to take advantage of these breakthroughs. Even after the Industrial Revolution had transformed the rest of the world, China continued to lag. Attempts to impose industrial technology onto the traditional culture initially proved disastrous. Mao Tse-tung's Great Leap Forward, for example, attempted to turn rural villages into backyard factories, a quixotic effort that not only failed to turn China into an industrial power, but ruined its existing economy.

The lesson of history is clear. Certain cultures are better suited to take advantage of advanced technologies than others. This ability (or inability) to take advantage of technology is likely to manifest itself in the culture's choice of leaders, and the development of its political structures. In this way, a culture can get trapped in a Catch-22 where it not only lacks the ability to adapt to new technology, but remains shackled in highly conservative institutions that almost reflexively fear anything new—especially technology that might enable or drive massive social changes.

What was true during the Industrial Revolution is also true today. For years, futurists such as Alvin Toffler have been talking about an "information revolution"—a change in technology that is as significant and fundamental as the Industrial Revolution of the nineteenth century.

According to this theory, the world is undergoing a profound transformation away from the industrial economy of the past. In an industrial economy, wealth comes from the ability to control money capital. Markets change slowly, favoring large and stable corporations. Information is now supposed to be a "new form of capital, one that is arguably more critical to the future of the American economy than money capital." In an information economy, wealth comes from the ability to manipulate and control information. Markets change swiftly, favoring nimble and adaptable corporations.

Just as China's conservative culture was unable to adapt to the Industrial Age, many corporations have corporate cultures that are ill-suited for the swiftly changing markets of the information age. Weighed down by bloated bureaucracies and hordes of middle managers, many of them can't move fast enough to remain competitive. Despite all the frantic attempts to reorganize, downsize, rightsize, outsource, reengineer, manage quality, and so forth, most corporate shake-ups fail, according to *The Wall Street Journal*. Even Hammer and Champy, authors of the bestseller *Reengineering the Corporation*, admit that as many as 70 percent of all reengineering campaigns fail. Executives and middle managers continue to cling to their hard-won authority and privileges. Employees dig in their heels and torpedo anything that seems to threaten the status quo. As a result, corporations continue to flounder, barely coping with the chaos.

Taken in proper perspective, this shouldn't surprise us. Traditional corporate culture evolved during a time when women weren't allowed to vote, slavery was legal, mass media was a broadside newspaper, and long-distance communication was a letter on a sailing ship. Most corporations are saddled with a business culture that belongs to a prior stage in our technological development.

As we shall see later in this book, the computerization of the working world has created a business environment that favors companies with decentralized, flexible cultures (such as Hewlett-Packard and Microsoft), putting companies with centralized, inflexible cultures (such as the Digital and IBM of the 1980s and early 1990s) at a definite disadvantage. And what's true about the computer industry is likely to prove true in other industries as the computerization of the office continues apace. Companies that plan to be successful in the future would do well to understand how the corporate culture of the Electronic Elite made these upstart companies so thoroughly undefeatable.

What Is Corporate Culture?

But I'm getting a little ahead of myself. I've been talking about corporate cultures without defining what I mean by the term. Let's start with the standard definition and then I'll give you my own, slightly modified, version.

The year 1982 saw the publication of an influential book entitled *Corporate Cultures*. This book explained how an organization's culture predetermines its employees' behavior. Authors Deal and Kennedy defined corporate culture as "a strong system of informal rules that spells out how people are to behave most of the time." One way I like to envision corporate culture is to think of it as the banks of a river. The behaviors in the corporation are like water that flows alongside those banks. Over time, these behaviors dig the channel deeper, reinforcing the culture so that it continues to reproduce the behaviors that led to success in the past, as shown in Figure 1.1.

Corporate Cultures focused on "values" as the primary element of corporate culture. The authors believed that the most important values of a culture were encapsulated in a corporation's motto. For example, the motto "IBM means service" reinforced IBM's dedication to the customer. The problem with this definition of corporate

FIGURE 1.1. *Culture Predetermines Behavior*

culture is that it doesn't explain why a company chooses a particular motto in the first place. Corporate mottoes are symbolic manifestations of a corporation's culture, but they don't define what the culture is all about any more than *E Pluribus Unum* explains what the culture of the United States is all about. To really understand corporate culture, we have to dig deeper.

According to my research and observation, a large part of any corporation's culture consists of the *cultural mindsets* that people use to evaluate the appropriateness of business behavior. A cultural mindset is a habitual image, metaphor, or paradigm that acts as an emotional and intellectual touchstone for determining what's "the right thing to do." To understand the concept of a cultural mindset more clearly, it helps to look outside the business world for a moment.

For the past 20 years, the U.S. government has been waging a so-called war against drugs. The phrase "war on drugs" is a specific manifestation of a cultural mindset that considers social action to be similar to the process of conducting warfare. This Social Action=Warfare mindset also finds expression in phrases like a "war on poverty," and a "war against illiteracy." The warlike nature of this cultural mindset appeals to our sense of urgency. It's intended to suggest to people that their elected officials will spare no effort to "win the war."

However, the Social Action=Warfare mindset carries some unintended baggage. Take the war on drugs. Couching antidrug activity in terms of militaristic attitudes sets the tone for the debate about the problem. It forces our society to focus attention on warlike "solutions," such as the funding of special police forces, stepped-up efforts to catch offshore smugglers, defoliant bombing of South American drug fields, and so forth. The warlike metaphor also virtually guarantees that comparatively little attention will be given to less warlike approaches to the problem, such as drug education and therapy for addicts. It also keeps our government from seriously considering alternative approaches such as decriminalization. Decriminalization may be a very bad idea for a number of reasons, but as long as the debate is framed inside a Social Action=Warfare mindset, the idea is almost unthinkable. Decriminalization would seem like "surrender," an admission that the "war" had been lost. This would remain true even though the ultimate goal—less social damage as a result of drug abuse—might be thus achieved.

In the same way, the cultural mindset of a corporation limits the kinds of strategies that it is willing to attempt. For example, a common cultural mindset in traditional corporations is that conducting business is similar to conducting warfare: Business=Battlefield. You see this mindset in action when you hear people say things like "nuking the competition" or "shooting the messenger" or "mustering the troops." Companies that have internalized the Business=Battlefield mindset are irresistibly drawn toward large, hierarchical, army-like organizational structures. Managers in such organizations are highly unlikely to effectively implement a scheme that requires low-level employees to make more decisions. Even though they may talk about "empowerment," managers in militaristic corporate cultures will tend to resist any attempt to turn employees into something other than "troops" whose business it is to "follow orders."

I once sat in on a meeting during which a consultant was presenting a reengineering plan to the management at a highly conservative, regimented, military-style corporation. One of the key points of the presentation was that the reengineering effort would "empower people." When the consultant began talking about this, the managers became restless and uncomfortable. The senior executive in the group stopped the presentation. "What exactly do you mean by 'empowers people'?" he asked the consultant. The consultant, sensing that he'd made a gafe, thought quickly. "It means that the reengineering will empower *management*," he replied coolly. "After all, managers are people, too." At this, the audience relaxed into their chairs and listened to the rest of the presentation with open hearts and minds, because it didn't conflict with their notion that employees were supposed to follow orders.

TRADITIONAL CORPORATE MINDSETS

The Business=Battlefield notion is an example of what I call a *traditional corporate mindset*. I consider it to be "traditional" because the Business=Battlefield idea evolved when factory owners during the Industrial Revolution needed a way to coordinate the activity of large numbers of people. The most effective model for this in the nineteenth century was the Napoleonic army. Napoleonic armies were controlled by a core of senior officers, had strong chains of command, dressed soldiers in standardized uniforms, and carefully segmented the activities of the troops into specialized functions. Early corporations mimicked these techniques, which is why most corporations today are run by executive "officers," have strong "chains of command," insist that the "troops" wear blue collars, and remain obsessed with job titles and job responsibilities.

The Business=Battlefield notion is one of six key cultural mindsets that make up the core of traditional corporate culture. This is the corporate culture that's prevalent in most companies today and is familiar to anybody who's worked in or around "big business" in the past 50 years. On the surface, traditional corporate culture is symbolized by the three-piece suits, fancy boardrooms, complicated organization charts, and a "manage by the numbers" attitude. Underneath lie the six key corporate mindsets summarized here:

1. *Business=Battlefield.* Business is a series of conflicts between companies inside a market, between departments inside a company, between groups inside an organization, between individuals in a group and (by extension) between customers and vendors. Resulting behaviors: Managers build big empires and "armies" of employees to fight the war. Managers order the "troops" around, while the troops wait around for "marching orders." Customers become territory to be conquered rather than potential partners, and the competition is demonized into the "enemy." Women, because supposedly they're not natural soldiers, are considered inappropriate for positions of authority.

2. *Corporation=Machine.* A corporation is a system in which employees are faceless cogs. Nobody is indispensable, and everybody is as replaceable as a spare part. Individual initiative, goals, and desires are considered to be completely subsumed by the demands of the corporate machine. Resulting behaviors: Managers create rigid organizations with rigid roles and rigid functions. Managers and workers alike become convinced that change is very difficult, similar to retooling a complicated machine. Managers are encouraged to think of themselves as "controllers" whose job it is to make sure that people follow the rules of the "system." Employees are treated in dehumanizing ways while the corporation centralizes control at the top.

3. *Management=Control.* The real job of the manager is to control employees' behaviors so that they do exactly what management wants them to do. Employees who disagree with a manager or refuse to do something are "insubordinate" and therefore dangerous. Resulting behaviors: Managers create organizations that can't adapt to new conditions because there are conflicting power structures, each of which is trying to "control" the corporation. Management gets involved in a supercharged political atmosphere where productive work becomes difficult. Individual initiative is killed in favor of a "let's wait and see what the boss says" mentality.

4. *Employee=Child.* Employees are too immature and foolish to be assigned real authority, and simply can't be trusted. If not restricted by a complicated rules and regulations, they'll steal a company blind. Resulting behaviors: Employees develop a deep and abiding resentment toward management. They refuse to do anything until they're certain that they won't get blamed if something goes wrong. Employees spend more time "covering their butts" than doing productive work. Employees only work when they're being watched, if then.

5. *Motivation=Fear.* Employees only work because they're afraid of getting fired. Managers must therefore use fear—fear of getting fired, fear of ridicule, fear of loss of privilege—to motivate people. Resulting behaviors: Employees and managers alike

become paralyzed, unable to make risky decisions or take coura-
geous action. Work becomes a loathsome experience filled with
truckling, ass-kissing, and compulsive corporate politicking.

6. *Change=Pain.* Change is seen as complicated and difficult.
Change is considered something that companies only undergo
if they're in desperate shape. Resulting behaviors: Reengineering, restructuring, and downsizing operations fail as people in
the organization torpedo the change efforts to avoid the pain
of change.

These six key traditional corporate mindsets, and their weaknesses in a computerized workplace, are described in more detail
later in this book.

Most people in business assume that these traditional corporate
mindsets simply reflect "The Way Things Really Are," when in
fact these habitual ways of thinking are merely mental filters for
interpreting business behavior. Just as the Social Action=Warfare
cultural mindset limits how our government is willing to approach
the drug problem, traditional corporate mindsets limit corporations to pursuing certain kinds of business strategies, *even if those
strategies no longer make sense under today's market conditions.*

For example, if you've been reading the business press over the
past 10 years, you've probably seen the overwhelming evidence that
centralized, monolithic organizations tend to be weaker and less
competitive than decentralized, team-based organizations. In spite
of this evidence, centralized, monolithic organizations often find
it next to impossible to transform themselves into decentralized,
team-based organizations, even through the use of well-regarded
corporate change methodologies such as Total Quality Management (TQM). According to a 1994 poll cited in *Fortune* magazine,
executives believe that less than one-third of TQM efforts are anything more than a "flop." The most frequently mentioned barriers
to change were "employee resistance and dysfunctional corporate
culture."

The consistent failure of corporate change attempts—even when
change is desperately needed—makes sense when you understand

the powerful influence that the six key traditional cultural mind-sets have on the subconscious attitudes of managers and employees alike. Any attempt to implement something like TQM is destined to fail if the management believes—at a gut level—that its function is to systematically use fear to manipulate the behavior of mentally inferior, childlike troops. Meaningful corporate transformation becomes even less likely if the people inside the dysfunctional organization are convinced—again, at a gut level—that any attempt to change the current system would be incredibly painful, involving loss of status, loss of salary, and (above all) loss of control. The subconscious influence of the cultural mindsets lock the status quo into place.

The effect of these six key traditional corporate mindsets is all the more pervasive because they reinforce one another, making it difficult to disbelieve in one without disbelieving in all the rest. I've run into this problem many times in my work as a strategic consultant.

I was once called in to help a company decide how to organize to compete for a newly developing high-tech market. My client's highly successful competition were structured as autonomous teams, with each team responsible for an individual product. This allowed them to bring products out with great rapidity. By contrast, my client was organized into broad, functional groups with vague, bureaucratic responsibilities—an organizational structure that had enormous problems getting a product out the door at all, never mind quickly. Although my client had racked up a series of impressive failures, I encountered an extraordinary amount of resistance when I recommended that my client restructure itself to develop more punch to the product teams.

The first objection was that "our system doesn't work that way." When I pointed out that their system could be changed, I ran into the second objection: "Our workers need management supervision." When I pointed out that their workers were, for the most part, highly educated professionals, the next objection was: "It would take too long to make major changes; we need to go after this market *now!*" When I pointed out that my client had failed in earlier attempts to address similar markets with its current structure, I found myself back at the original objection: "Our system just doesn't work that way."

Trying to get this company to make necessary operational changes was like trying to cut off hydra heads—every time one objection was laid to rest, another sprang up to take its place. The reason for my client's resistance was that its management was completely dominated by three corporate mindsets: Corporation=Machine, Employee=Child, and Change=Pain. Because of this highly emotional attachment, the company was unable to visualize or effectively implement the changes needed to be successful in its target market. Under the circumstances, the best that could be expected from the company was an attempt to make current strategies more cost-effective. So rather than fixing the real problem, the company merely began a series of debilitating downsizes, which resulted in short-term profitability and long-term market failure.

ELECTRONIC ELITE CORPORATE MINDSETS

By contrast, some organizations have little difficulty adapting to new market conditions. In particular, the corporations of the Electronic Elite had proven to be extremely nimble in this regard. To discover the reason for this, I had studied their organizational structure and business models, but I still wasn't able to put my finger on what was really different about these companies. I did know, however, that *something* had to be very different, because these companies were not only trouncing the traditional computer vendors, they were breaking major records for business growth and success.

COMPAQ, for example, shipped its first computer in 1982, and in 1983 (the year it went public), it recorded sales of $111 million—unprecedented growth for a start-up. COMPAQ then went on to top the $2 billion mark within six years. Dell Computers, run by boy-genius Michael Dell, grew from a $30,000 start-up in 1984 to a $3 billion corporation in 10 years, making it one of the fastest-growing companies in the Fortune 500. Microsoft has done a truly spectacular job creating wealth for its investors. Since it went public, Microsoft stock has been returning an average 59 percent yearly growth, enough to turn a $15,000 investment in 1986 into a cool $1 million by 1995. There was something unique about these companies and, by extension, something unique about the people who led them.

I've already mentioned that the Electronic Elite attribute the success of their companies to their powerful corporate cultures. During my conversations with the Electronic Elite, I started listening, very carefully, for clues that might lead me to identify the specific nature of this new culture. I began noticing that the vocabulary of the Electronic Elite differed from that of traditional business leaders. For example, in the many hours of business talk, I *never* heard the "shoot-em-up," "destroy the competition," "order out the troops" tough talk that had become so familiar to me in my contacts with top management of other corporations. Instead, the Electronic Elite used different words, drew different analogies, made different comparisons.

As I probed at their strategies and attitudes I began to perceive speech patterns that suggested corporate mindsets that were very different from the ones that provided the cultural framework for the typical "old school" company. I was able to see an important contrast between the traditional corporate mindsets (that I knew so well from my prior experiences) and the images, metaphors, and mindsets that the Electronic Elite were using. It eventually became clear to me that the corporate culture of the Electronic Elite represented a complete overthrow of the interlocked corporate mindsets that defined and delimited the business behaviors of the past. The new corporate culture represented a revolutionary new framework for business behavior, a framework that had evolved in response to the Information Revolution, just as the old corporate mindsets had evolved in response to the Industrial Revolution. These six new mindsets are summarized here:

1. *Business=Ecosystem.* The business world is made up of symbiotic relationships formed to exploit market niches. The company

that is the most diverse is the most likely to thrive. Business result: Companies adapt quickly to new market conditions, tend to hire and promote people with different backgrounds and thought processes, and form interesting partnerships with other companies.

2. *Corporation=Community.* A company is a collection of individuals with individual hopes and dreams that are connected to their organization's higher purpose. Business result: Employees dedicate themselves to the goals of the organization and truly enjoy contributing to their own success, the success of their peers, and the success of the community at large.

3. *Management=Service.* A manager's job is to set a direction and to obtain the resources that employees need to get the job done. Management wants to "lead" rather than "run" the organization. Business result: Decision making takes place at the "lowest" level of the company. Teams form their own rules and direction without interference from corporate headquarters.

4. *Employee=Peer.* Every employee is hired—regardless of position—as if he or she were the most important person in the company. Excellence is expected and encouraged everywhere from the loading dock to the boardroom. Business result: Employees at all levels take charge of their own destinies. A spirit of friendly competition develops to see who can serve the organization the best.

5. *Motivation=Vision.* People know where they're going and are amply rewarded when they get there, so the process of working is filled with energy, enthusiasm, and humor. Business result: Employees work hard, not out of obligation or out of fear, but because they believe in the organization's goals, truly enjoy what they're doing, and know that they'll share in the profits.

6. *Change=Growth.* Change is a desirable thing because it's part of the process of adapting to new market conditions and growing into new levels of success. Business result: Employees and organization embrace new ideas, new ways of doing business, and new ways of making profit.

These six corporate mindsets combine to create the cultural framework for companies that are decentralized, trusting, empowering, informal and flexible, rather than centralized, bureaucratic, controlling, formal, and rigid. Just as the traditional corporate mindsets reinforce one another, Electronic Elite corporate mindsets are interlocked and mutually supportive. The Change=Growth mindset, for example, fits exactly with the notion that Business=Ecosystem. Similarly, the Employee=Peer mindset naturally leads managers away from controlling behaviors and into an attitude of serving the organization (Management=Service).

These six key corporate mindsets of the Electronic Elite are described in detail later in this book, along with the specific strategies that the Electronic Elite use to turn these mindsets into competitive advantages. These six key mindsets (and the strategies they support) result in a productive, yet humane workplace that emphasizes freedom, initiative, and fun, rather than obedience, conformity, and fear. In my opinion, this new corporate culture represents a giant leap forward in the evolution of the American corporation.

This is not to say that the companies of the Electronic Elite are perfect. Far from it. Working in these companies can be frustrating. The hours can be long and there's often a great deal of internal competition. As in all human institutions, the reality sometimes falls short of the ideal.

Still, the people who work in these environments are, by and large, excited and fascinated by their careers. As I've spoken with the employees in these companies, I can't tell you the number of times I've heard, "I really love working here" or "this is a great place to work." And this isn't just from the executives, it's from the people who answer the telephones, program the computers, cart boxes on the loading dock, or field customer requests.

This positive attitude reflects and reinforces the success that the companies of the Electronic Elite have enjoyed as they've grown into some of the most powerful and influential companies in the world. Both the attitude and the success are, as we shall see, the natural and inevitable results of the new cultural mindsets.

Merely having an Electronic Elite corporate culture doesn't guarantee success. There are no guarantees, and while an Elite corporate culture may provide a powerful advantage against an old-school, traditional competitor, something more is needed when competitors both have highly evolved Elite cultures. It's one thing to take on a lumbering behemoth like IBM; it's quite another thing to take on a nimble giant like Microsoft.

However, regardless of the competition, one of the best ways to remain competitive is to learn and emulate the beliefs and behaviors of successful organizations. Therefore, in the next six chapters of this book, we'll look at how the six key cultural mindsets have allowed the Electronic Elite to compete, and win, inside one of the fastest moving and dynamic markets in the world.

Chapter Two

Business Is an Ecosystem

The first and most important mindset of the Electronic Elite is that the process of doing business is similar to guiding and directing the processes of nature: Business is like an ecosystem.

An ecosystem is a community of living organisms that have complex and finely balanced symbiotic relationships. While the members often compete for resources, they must always maintain the balance. The death of a predator species, for example, might cause the destruction of an entire ecosystem through overgrazing by herbivores. Ecosystems that are homogenous—that contain only a few species—are fragile. Any unusual event will upset the balance. Ecosystems that are diverse and contain a variety of species are robust and more likely to remain viable over long periods.

According to the Electronic Elite, that's pretty much how the business world works. A market is a complex set of relationships between customers, vendors, suppliers, and competitors. These relationships are finely balanced and can include very large companies—like Microsoft—and very small companies, like your local computer store. Corporations can be regarded as ecosystems as well. Those that have a lot of "biological diversity," a greater variety of people and products, are more likely to thrive than monolithic, single-product companies that are composed of people who think and act the same.

The Business=Ecosystem mindset is nothing new. The concept that economic systems paralleled biological systems had been bouncing around academia for some years before it was developed and described in 1990 by Michael Rothschild in the book *Bionomics: Economy as Ecosystem*. The Electronic Elite, however, are the first business leaders to take this new mindset entirely to heart.

One high-tech company that has an ecological view of business is Novell. When Novell was founded in 1980, it was a tiny organization making add-on boards for those few hobbyists who were building personal computers at the time. Novell soon began concentrating on software networks, the computer technology that connects personal computers. To remain competitive and to stay on the edge of technological innovation, Novell grew by acquiring and merging with other technology companies.

Rather than trying to create a single, monolithic organization, former Novell CEO Ray Noorda let these different businesses pursue strategies and tactics that made sense for their products. This gave the company a robust diversity that made it possible to adapt to changes in the marketplace. When economic conditions or technical breakthroughs rendered one Novell group less successful, another Novell group benefited. The strategy paid off. From a tiny start-up in 1980, Novell's 1994 revenues climbed to over $1 billion, and the company employed over 4,000 people.

The CEO of Novell today is Bob Frankenberg. A serious, light-haired leader with an engineer's wire-rim glasses, Bob has a wry, understated sense of humor about the ins and outs of the computer industry. Formerly an executive at Hewlett-Packard, Bob Frankenberg considers the diversity of Novell's organization a major reason that Novell is such a powerful competitor. During our conversation, Bob explained:

> If you become too homogeneous, you can become very introspective and find yourself without the diversity that's necessary for evolution when a market changes or when a new set of capabilities emerge. All of the studies of evolution point out that the diversity of a given population is one of the prime factors required for survival, and so, becoming too homogeneous is very dangerous.

Novell has roots in 23 different companies. We have different ways of developing . . . . We've got a wide range of approaches. I think that if we don't continue to do that, as conditions shift (and in this business, conditions shift very frequently), there's a danger of not surviving; but most important, I think we would miss some of the great opportunities as they emerge.

When Bob talks about evolution and diversity, he's revealing the influence that the Business=Ecosystem mindset has on his strategic thinking. This mindset allows Novell to behave in ways that are totally foreign to run-of-the-mill traditional companies, which tend to view business as a battlefield.

THE TRADITIONAL MINDSET: BUSINESS=BATTLEFIELD

Unlike the Electronic Elite, many traditional business leaders have a militaristic view of the way the business world works. A glance at the titles of popular business books—*Marketing Warfare, Leadership Secrets of Attila the Hun, Guerrilla PR*—offer ample testimony for this widely held viewpoint. We're told that we must imitate generals and warlords if we want to be successful managers. Taking all this to heart, many executives talk as if they were planning the next world war:

This product will do major damage in the marketplace! We've armed our sales force. We've targeted the right set of customers! The new ad campaign will explode into the territories! This is going to be a major victory! Our troops are ready!

Yes, Virginia, some people really talk like this. And it would just be macho rhetoric if it weren't that it symbolizes a general attitude that's frequently ineffective in today's fast-moving markets. We really can't blame traditional executives for thinking this way because their beliefs are deeply embedded in their corporate culture. In the typical corporation, power is concentrated at the top, where the commander in chief (chief executive officer) is surrounded by a general staff (corporate officers), who give orders to lesser officers (vice presidents, directors, etc.), who give orders to the line officers (line managers), who give orders to the troops (employees). These orders *must* be obeyed; failure to do so (insubordination) results in court-martial (disciplinary action) or death (termination).

Although the analogies between business and warfare seem timeless, people didn't always connect them. In the Middle Ages, for example, warfare was the occupation of dukes and princes, and only commoners and knaves soiled their hands with commerce. In fact, if you had suggested to a knight that business was the same thing as warfare, he probably would have gently corrected you by separating your head from your shoulders. In the eighteenth century, it was the other way around. Merchant princes hobnobbed with dukes and kings, while warfare was a dirty business best left to mercenaries, wastrels, and cutthroats.

Today, however, many companies resonate with warlike attitudes. And if a company's executives really believe that business is warfare, then that dogma will be reflected in nearly everything that goes on inside the corporation. Strategies that don't fit the dogma—regardless of their potential for success—will be rejected because they are literally "unthinkable." For example, executives who believe that business is a battlefield will almost inevitably assume that victory in business goes to the largest "army" and they'll build large, complicated departments stuffed full of people and resources. Even when customers would be better served by a smaller, more focused effort, there will be an overwhelming drive to build a massive corporate "army" that's "strong" and ready to "fight."

That was one of the problems that IBM had, according to a former IBM vice president:

> What most big companies need is more decentralization. The best structure is to become a collection of small businesses. That's hard for big companies, because executives don't want to think about anything that isn't a $100 million business. Yet that's exactly how Microsoft and Intel got started—as small companies. Big companies approach developing markets in exactly the wrong way. Since everything they're interested in is supposed to be a $100 million business, they invest in enough infrastructure to

make it a $100 million business. But that's the last thing that you want to do, because now you have a cost structure that undercuts your profitability and a bureaucracy that keeps the business from adapting to the market.

In addition to building large organizational empires, military-minded managers find it all too easy to become control freaks. Because they see themselves as generals and officers, they *tell* people what to do. They think that good employees should shut up and follow orders. This behavior destroys initiative as people wait around for top management to make decisions. And because top management is often the most isolated from the customer, the company loses track of what's needed in the marketplace. Further, the business=battlefield mentality makes it impossible to put the decision making where it belongs—at the lowest level of the organization.

Military thinking also distances employees from their customers. To the militaristic company, customers are, at best, faceless territory to be "targeted" and "captured" with marketing and sales "campaigns." This strategy discourages the viewing of customers as living, breathing human beings with opinions, interests, and concerns of their own.

This attitude can deeply offend customers. On a recent plane trip, I sat next to the vice president of a large media company. He told me a story about a salesperson who had given a sales pitch for a new computer system. The salesperson kept using the word "targeted": The product was "targeted" for the media industry, the ad campaign was "targeted" at new customers, sales resources had been "targeted" in this geographic area, and so forth. Finally the VP got fed up and threw the guy out. "I felt like he was aiming a #@&*! gun at my head," the VP confided to me. "Not once did he bother to tell me how his product would help me make more money."

Military-minded companies often abuse customers in their quest for "victory." Since "all's fair in war," they feel free to use any means—fair or foul—to "win." This was brought home to me when my mother, a top salesperson for a cosmetics firm, got a new manager. He was a typical corporate Rambo, forever giving the salespeople pep talks about "hating" the competition, "blasting them out of the water," and "doing major damage in the region." This tough talk translated into pushing distributors to order products that they didn't need so that the sales manager would have a "winning" quarterly report. The distributors, naturally, began to order less, which drove the sales manager crazy. He intensified his pep talks. One day he ended with the instruction, "So let's rape and pillage, and leave no wounded!" At this, my mother raised her hand. "Excuse me, sir, could you clarify a point, please?" "Certainly." "Who, exactly, do you want us to rape?" she asked, her voice dripping honey. She took early retirement a few weeks later.

Which brings up another issue. The whole military concept, with its buddy-buddy, band-of-brothers, shoot-'em-up consciousness seems ludicrous to many women. Not having spent their childhood playing soldiers in the sandbox, many women find it pretty ridiculous that a bunch of grown men can act as if their boring meetings and dry-as-dust ideas were high adventure and global conflict.

The militaristic company almost always discriminates against women. From time immemorial, warfare has been a male pastime, and though women have often fought and died in wars, they're generally considered second-class soldiers. Men who think that executives should be generals in three-piece suits find it extraordinarily difficult to envision a woman in a position of power. This is short-sighted, because women are capable of the highest performance at all levels of business activity. Military thinking, which disqualifies women from being full contributors, weakens organizations by stripping them of a valuable source of new ideas and insight.

The Electronic Elite don't buy into the Business=Battlefield mindset because they know that it's inconsistent with the kind of business behaviors that produce success in today's marketplace. For example, Frank Ingari is the president of Shiva, a Massachusetts-based company that makes software for mobile computers. Frank used to be the head of marketing at Lotus and was responsible for much of the success of the Lotus 1-2-3 spreadsheet. Frank is a soft-spoken and thoughtful man, a calm rather than dynamic leader. Lest you think that he's dull, however, you should know that he's been known to play in a rock 'n' roll band called Look and Feel, whose members are the heads of several local software firms. In the year and a half he's been at Shiva, he's been able to shepherd the company to its first public stock offering, and the company continues to grow. It was Frank Ingari who made it clear to me that he and his peers considered the Business=Battlefield mindset to be dysfunctional. Here's what he said:

> I simply won't tolerate disrespect of people. That's a basic value with me. If people have integrity and a sense of wholeness, then there's no excuse for treating each other with disrespect—sexism, ageism, any kind of discrimination, any kind of militaristic behavior. "I am the pooh–bah and I am ordering you to do the following things." I don't buy that at all. My disbelief in militaristic power doesn't mean that I don't use power. There are many times where I've said, "Hey, this is what we're going to do." But I don't just tell my direct report we're doing it and leave it at that. I'll call all the employees into a room, explain the rationale; I'll tell them everything. I'll tell them the financials, what I was thinking, my concerns, what I weighed, the decision I made, who's accountable for the decision—usually me—whether or not I'm open to entertaining any debate. So, it's not that you don't direct, but you treat people with respect even when you direct. My goal in that communication is not going to be to tell you that this isn't my fault, and you should just do what I'm telling you. I'm going to try to get you to understand why this happened, and if I take a black eye, well, okay, I'm human too. I'm going to make mistakes.

One of the few elements of the Business=Battlefield way of thinking that's still present in the companies of the Electronic Elite are the military-style job titles (such as CEO). However, when one of the Electronic Elite tells you that he or she is a chief executive officer, there's always a bit of a twinkle in the eye or a lift of one eyebrow, just to let you know that you shouldn't take the title too seriously. You get the impression that the typical Electronic

Elite CEO would just as soon be called head gardener or chief cook and bottle washer, if it weren't that the financial community won't talk to you unless you have a fancy nineteenth-century title on your business card.

The Electronic Elite prefer the Business=Ecosystem mindset, which drives an entirely different set of business behaviors from the Business=Battlefield mindset, as shown in Table 2.1.

The behavior that's driven by the Business=Ecosystem mindset seems insane by those who hold the battlefield viewpoint. In an army, diversity makes for a rabble; starting small seems a recipe for getting crushed; and, in the end, what's a battle without winners and losers? Conversely, militaristic behavior is viewed as insane by followers of the ecosystem mindset. Uniformity means that organizations can't adapt; blitzing markets seems like pulling up young plants to make them grow faster; and conflict just seems like so much wasted effort.

The dominant mindsets inside an organization inevitably influence the way the people of that organization try to solve a problem or take advantage of a market opportunity. The battlefield mindset leads companies to behave in ways that may have made sense in the past, but that are recipes for failure today. To illustrate this,

TABLE 2.1. *Comparison of Battlefield and Ecosystem Mindsets*

BUSINESS=BATTLEFIELD	BUSINESS=ECOSYSTEM
Uniformity. A strong organization is one where everyone dresses the same, shares the same background, and follows corporate standards.	*Diversity.* A strong organization is diverse, containing a wide variety of opinions, ideas, products, and sales channels.
Cash Cows. The primary goal of every organization is to defensively protect profitable revenue streams, even if it means forgoing new opportunities.	*Generations.* The goal of every organization is to create new products, which obsolete currently profitable products that the organization is already selling.
Conflict. Business is essentially a win-lose proposition. It's a zero-sum game where competitors, and even customers, are enemies.	*Symbiosis.* Business is a set of win-win relationships, not only between customers, vendors, and suppliers, but even among "competitors."

let's look at different ways that an Electronic Elite company, Novell, and an older, more traditional minicomputer vendor, Digital, both attempted to dominate the market for computer networks.

CASE STUDY: NOVELL AND DIGITAL STRIVE FOR THE NETWORK MARKET

It was 1980. The personal computer was considered more of a toy for hobbyists than a viable computing platform, but exciting things were starting to happen in the computer industry. Unbeknownst to all at the time, the era of the centralized mainframe was drawing to a close, even though most computers that year were still large mainframes that sat safely inside temperature-controlled rooms at corporate headquarters. Anyone who wanted to access the precious computing resources of the mainframes had to beg corporate bureaucrats for rental time. To satisfy this growing need, IBM and the other mainframe manufacturers were trying to build *bigger* and faster machines, in the hopes that they would be able to serve a greater number of people.

At the same time, another group of computer vendors were building minicomputers, scaled-down versions of the giant mainframes. Unlike the mainframes, which required a special environment, minicomputers could be installed virtually anywhere. This meant that an individual department or division could purchase its own computer, making it unnecessary to access the computers at corporate headquarters.

Digital Equipment Corporation (Digital) was the unquestioned leader in minicomputer technology. What made Digital's computers particularly useful was that they were easy to configure into networks. This meant that the computers in different departments not only could share data, but could cooperate with each other to solve difficult computing tasks.

There were many reasons why Digital's networking idea made sense. Networking allowed companies to distribute computer power away from corporate headquarters. People at a manufacturing center, for example, could keep track of inventory using a computer that was located inside the plant. This computer could, in turn, be connected to another machine in the accounting department that helped the purchasing department order supplies; which then could be connected to a third computer, on which engineers could design the next product to be manufactured. The network freed people in different parts of the company to own their own "departmental" computer while still sharing important data with other departments.

Networking minicomputers had advantages over the giant mainframes. If the mainframe had a problem, all the departments and divisions that depended on it would lose their access to computing power. A system crash or other error could easily cause havoc throughout the entire company, bringing productivity to a gut-wrenching halt. With a Digital-style network, on the other hand, if one of the computers had a problem, the rest could go on their merry way; only the department with the "sick" computer suffered. While this might prove inconvenient to the affected department, it was certainly less likely to bring the entire company to its knees. In many cases, people in the affected department were able to use the computers in the other departments while their own computer was getting fixed. Thus, a Digital network could be both safer and more cost-effective.

Enter the personal computer. The PC, with its built-in microprocessor and communications capability, was the perfect vehicle for creating new computer networks. Just as Digital's minicomputers had made it possible to build networks, the personal computer made it possible to build low-cost networks using even smaller components. This made many of the advantages of the Digital-style network available to a much larger group of people, and at a much lower cost.

Here was a once-in-a-decade opportunity for Digital, and if the company had rewritten its networking software so that it would run on the personal computer, Digital could have captured the rapidly growing market for PC-based networks. Digital was, after all, the acknowledged leader in networking software. Other computer vendors had competing products, but none of them were as flexible, useful, practical, and stable as those that Digital made. Digital also had hundreds of thousands of loyal customers who would have flocked to buy a PC network built by Digital.

Digital did not respond to the challenge, however. Rather than embracing the personal computer and rewriting its software to run on them, Digital clung to its minicomputers. It made some half-hearted attempts to include personal computers as part of their minicomputer-based networks, but that wasn't what customers wanted. As a result, despite Digital's dominance of the networking market, Novell was easily able to capture market share to the point where, today, Novell owns two-thirds of the market for networks. Digital, once the market leader, wanders around in the basement with single-digit shares.

How could Digital, which practically invented networking, become so irrelevant, so quickly? What happened was an almost classic series of blunders on Digital's part, and Novell grew at Digital's expense because it approached the business of making money in a very different way:

- *Business Model.* Novell, like Digital, had originally been a hardware vendor. However, Novell began focusing on software when it became clear that it was more profitable to sell software than hardware, even though this required a major change in Novell's business model and method of operation. Digital, on the other hand, continued building and selling hardware based on the same business model that they'd been using for the past 20 years. Novell's culture was flexible; Digital's was not.
- *Product Strategy.* Although the sales figures for personal computer networks were initially small, Novell stayed focused on this market niche, believing that it would continue to grow over time. Digital, on the other hand, continued to tap what it regarded as the more established market for minicomputer-based networks. This limited the appeal of Digital's networks to those people who wanted to buy Digital's proprietary products. Novell's culture searched for growing market niches; Digital's languished in a dying one.

- *Channel Strategy.* Digital sold the majority of its networks directly to customers, providing them with hardware, software, installation, and support—a "one-stop shop." Novell, on the other hand, concentrated on software, which it sold through value-added resellers (VARs)—local, privately owned companies. Where Digital tried to capture all the profit for itself, Novell shared the profit with its small-scale partners. Novell's culture encouraged this kind of symbiotic relationship; Digital's tended to exclude outsiders as if they were "enemies."

In other words, Novell adapted to new market conditions, while Digital kept doing the same things that had made it successful in the past, even though they were no longer producing success.

Digital's inability to adapt wasn't the result of management stupidity; the company had recruited the brightest and best from the leading management schools. And it certainly wasn't caused by a lack of technical expertise; Digital was filled with engineers such as David Cutler, who today is the architect of Microsoft's advanced networking operating system, Windows NT.

If it wasn't a lack of management brainpower or technical expertise that caused Digital to blunder so consistently, what was it? The answer is that Digital suffered from staying in the confines of a corporate culture that was not evolving apace with the fast-moving markets of the Information Age. This rendered Digital's management incapable of making the kind of clever moves that the upstart Novell found so natural. Digital was constrained by cultural insistence on viewing networking in one way. Digital's culture didn't provide the framework for a Novell-like strategy; instead, it limited its managers' choices to strategies that had worked in the past but that proved increasingly ineffective as time went on. Even when the ineffectiveness of the ingrained system was amply reflected in Digital's declining profitability, the company continued to do the same things, pursuing the same strategies, like a clockwork doll on overdrive.

Digital essentially was hypnotized—and thus crippled—by the Business=Battlefield way of looking at the world. For example, it was not unusual in the Digital of the 1980s for managers to give presentations that featured pictures of tanks, battleships, and fighter planes meant to represent different products, companies, and organizations. Military vocabulary permeated the company. People didn't design marketing strategies, they "launched campaigns." These campaigns had militaristic names like "Rolling Thunder" (named after the bombing campaign during the Vietnam War) or "Top Gun" (named after the popular Tom Cruise movie). And this kind of talk wasn't limited to managers. Among the "troops" (workers were always troops), it was popular to say that a person who had been criticized during a meeting had been "blown away," "massacred," or "nuked out of existence." A common greeting in the hallway was "how goes the battle?"—a greeting often accompanied by fingers shaped in the form of guns and aimed at one another.

The warlike images, vocabulary, and hand gestures were surface manifestations of the internal processes of the organization. Given the fascination with the battlefield mindset, it was inevitable that Digital would evolve toward ever more bureaucratic and stable organizational structures, with direct lines of command and executives who were determined to "run" the company.

Indeed, that is exactly what happened at Digital. The company's 1980s management opted for an organizational structure in which all the employees with a particular expertise were grouped together. Thus, there was a massive engineering group, a massive marketing group, and a massive sales group, each responsible for *all* of Digital's products and services. Under this kind of organizational structure, Digital employees naturally felt that their primary loyalty was to their functional discipline. Getting products out the door became secondary to making certain that corporate rules and regulations were followed. To be fair, the Digital of the mid-1990s is somewhat different from the Digital of the past. It's no longer as monolithic as it once was, and there are many indications that the company is trying to behave in new ways.

However, during the critical years that it was competing with Digital, Novell was enjoying an organizational structure based on the ecosystem mindset. Each product group had the resources and decision-making power to go after the market for that group's products. Rather than trying to *control* the process, Novell's top management *coordinated* activities and encouraged peer-to-peer cooperation between product groups, as shown in Figure 2.1. This allowed Novell employees to look at the market in a way that made them more nimble, more flexible, and better able to take advantage of opportunities and market changes. Novell CEO Bob Frankenberg commented:

> If you looked at some of the older computer companies or some of the ones that haven't made the transition, what you saw were these giant hierarchies. That was one of Digital's problems, for example. It had a functional organization, and all of the development was in one organization, all of the marketing was in another. Faster, more fleet-footed competitors, who structured themselves into small businesses yet stayed tied to the right kind of communication and information systems, were able to outrun Digital.

In addition to promoting different organizational structures, the Business=Ecosystem mindset encourages companies to follow three important corporate strategies. Understand these strategies and why they're effective and you'll be that much closer to making the power of the ecosystem mindset work for your organization. These strategies are:

- Encourage diversity.
- Launch new generations.
- Build symbiotic relationships.

Let's see how these strategies work for the Electronic Elite.

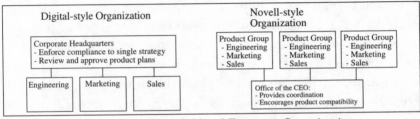

FIGURE 2.1. *Battlefield and Ecosystem Organizations*

Strategy 1: Encourage Diversity

Earlier in this chapter, we learned how Novell's CEO Bob Frankenberg values the diversity of his organization. He sees Novell's different businesses as important to Novell's future survival. Participating in a number of different businesses, with a variety of business models, makes Novell a stronger company, according to Bob. It makes the company far less likely to be damaged by a major shift in market trends and provides fresh alternatives for making money. Bob explained:

> I have a strong belief in what I call tight and loose. A few things are held very tightly but a lot of freedom is given to do what's needed. One of the tight elements is a set of objectives that we agree on. We come to agreement on what we're going to accomplish in each of the business groups. The other thing that we consider important is having the communication abilities to move information around so bright people can make good decisions based on the best information that we can get to them. We treat people with respect and hire the very best people. Beyond that, we've got a wide range of approaches.

Thus, while Novell's strategic direction comes from a "big picture" view of where the company needs to go, the implementation details, business model, and approach are determined by the people responsible for executing the specific parts of the overall plan. Novell maintains diversity, while being focused enough to keep from straying into inappropriate or unprofitable markets.

The devotion of the Electronic Elite to diversity spills over into the kind of personnel decisions that they make. When you visit the companies of the Electronic Elite, you immediately notice that they are filled with people from different social, racial, and cultural backgrounds. And there are more women in positions of responsibility than in most traditional companies. This is no accident. Neither is it the result of altruism or a sense of social conscience. On the contrary, the Electronic Elite value personnel diversity because they know that it's critical to the continuing process of innovation.

One company with a great history of innovation is Lotus Development Corporation. Lotus grew to be one of the largest software companies in the world by selling what's arguably the most popular personal productivity software of all time—the 1-2-3 spreadsheet. While 1-2-3 is still a big seller for Lotus, much of the company's energy today is spent developing groupware products like Lotus Notes. Notes allows people to share documents, comments, databases, and applications across a network. It's an amazing productivity tool that can help people manage projects even when those people are thousands of miles apart. The Notes product is a major reason that IBM recently purchased Lotus (as part of a hostile takeover) for $3.5 billion, the largest amount ever paid for a software company.

The CEO who shepherded Lotus for the past decade or so has been Jim Manzi. Jim left Lotus soon after the IBM takeover, but few question that he was instrumental in Lotus's rapid growth in the 1980s and early 1990s. He's outspoken and abrupt, the kind of person that people either love or hate. Those who love him say that he's an inspirational leader who guided Lotus into new markets. Those who hate him say that he's demanding and impatient. One of the questions I asked Jim was how he viewed the issue of diversity in the workplace. His response was, in my opinion, acutely representative of the way that the Electronic Elite perceive this important issue:

> I have no interest in being politically correct, which I find basically an obnoxious concept. However, there is a shared point of view at Lotus that a diverse culture—meaning people of different backgrounds and particularly people with different cognitive skills—makes for a better corporate culture, better products, and better service. These people bring different perspectives to a common problem, as opposed to having cookie-cutter white men of the same age and cultural background. A diverse culture is a lot more interesting for everybody, and this reflects in the kind of products that get built.

It's difficult to imagine a viewpoint that's further from that of the traditional CEO. In general, corporate America has had to be dragged kicking and screaming into accepting minorities and women. Despite years of apparent progress, the "glass ceiling" remains a formidable barrier to people who don't fit the mold of the white male leader.

The Electronic Elite believe this state of affairs is absurd. They don't have to be convinced with quotas and arm-twisting to accept a diversity of personnel into the workplace. On the contrary. They *embrace* it. For the Electronic Elite, the issue of diversity isn't one of fairness or some other moral abstraction. Diversity is simply a survival issue. The Electronic Elite can't afford a uniformity of thought that's so characteristic of the traditional corporation, because it's the kiss of death in today's quick-changing marketplace.

Being successful in the Information Age requires a very creative company building exciting new products quickly and effectively, forging new sales channels in a matter of months, and helping customers discover new ways to use new products. Just as the most robust ecosystems are those that contain the greatest variety of lifeforms, the most creative companies are those that enjoy the greatest diversity of viewpoints.

One member of the Electronic Elite who can vouch for this is Safi Qureshey, the Chairman of AST Research, Inc. Founded in 1980, when three Asian-born engineers in California decided to start a high-tech consulting business inside a garage, AST today is one of the top 10 manufacturers of personal computers in the world. Safi is a dynamic, restless individual, well known for his ability to conduct business around the clock, while his global organization builds and sells products at facilities around the world. Safi had this to say about diversity in his organization:

> If we were primarily addressing one market—let's say the North American market—it would have been OK to be just a homogeneous organization. But, we have a major presence in Europe, and we have a major presence in the Far East, especially in China and Hong Kong, where we are number one in market share by a wide margin. So, we are operating in different cultures and different regions, and having the talent and the management expertise, and understanding the cultural differences makes us a better partner

and a better supplier to those markets. We are not just taking a U.S.-centric view of the world. My own background—I come from a developing country—makes me a little bit more sensitive to the cultural differences. Whether I'm sitting in China or in Australia, or anywhere else, I can put myself in the shoes of the people I'm talking to.

Another indication of the Electronic Elite's commitment to diversity is the high percentage of key management positions held by women in these companies. Two of the most important software companies in the industry (AutoDesk and Ask Computing) are headed or were founded by women, and it's extremely common to see women in senior vice president roles or running major divisions inside Electronic Elite organizations. And, increasingly, women are starting their own high-tech companies.

Ann Winblad was one of the first women to found a software company. She is a pixieish blonde who has been a mentor to an entire generation of software CEOs. In 1976, Ann cofounded Open System, Inc., a top-selling accounting software supplier. Beginning with a $500 investment, she operated the company profitably for six years and ultimately sold the company in 1983 for $15.1 million. Today, Ann is a partner at Hummer Winblad Venture Partners, a $95 million software-only fund that she formed with John Hummer in 1989. Ann pointed out that of the dozen or so companies she featured in her latest brochure, three had women as CEOs or cofounders. But she pointed out:

The fact that they were women had nothing to do with the decision. The software industry is a meritocracy. We back the people with the best ideas.

That's exactly how the rest of the Electronic Elite view diversity. They hire the best people, and the best people are those with a fresh perspective.

Getting back to Novell, the company very wisely abandoned networking hardware in favor of a focus on networking software, even though this meant changing their entire business model, and not just because software was cheaper to manufacture and had higher margins than hardware. Novell software was designed to run on personal computers supplied by many different hardware vendors. When the cost of personal computer hardware dropped, it created an enormous demand for accompanying software. Novell was positioned perfectly to take advantage of this trend, and it was able to make the move into software because its management included people from different backgrounds and different companies. From the start, it was a diverse company, composed of many different people with a variety of ways of viewing the computer industry.

Digital's managers, on the other hand, clung to their tried-and-true business model. Most of Digital's management had been trained to design, manufacture, and sell hardware. Digital's management lacked the diversity of opinion and experience that would have enabled them to see future opportunities and accept the challenge to alter their way of doing business. Digital's management, consciously or unconsciously, was culturally driven toward greater regimentation, resembling the army that it was using as a model for good business practice.

Digital's executives, for all their brilliance, were cut from the same cloth. Novell, by contrast, with access to the softer and more flexible ecosystem mindset, had a tradition of encouraging diversity. This stood them in good stead when they needed to change their business model to take advantage of new opportunities.

There is another aspect to making the most of opportunities: having the right product at the right time. To achieve this, the Electronic Elite utilize another ecological strategy, allowing a new generation of products to become prominent when the time is right.

STRATEGY 2: LAUNCH NEW GENERATIONS

In an ecosystem, lifeforms survive through a process of reproduction. Each generation begets the next generation, thus ensuring the survival of the species. There's a cycle to life, a growth and decline of each generation. The Electronic Elite view their products in much the same way. They see products as having a relatively short lifetime, believing that even the most successful product of today is destined to be replaced by a next-generation product.

Carol Bartz is the CEO of AutoDesk, a wildly successful California-based software company that makes the world's most popular computer-aided design (CAD) package. As the head of one of the largest personal computer software companies in the world, Carol is arguably the most powerful woman in the computer industry. She's also a leader in public opinion and acts as a role model for many women in the computer industry. Carol explained the all-important notion of generations in high-tech products:

> You can't be afraid to obsolete your current products. You have to be very aggressive about taking a winning product and being ready to declare it obsolete, just when it's started to win. For example, in the hardware business, before you even introduce your product, you have to be readying its cost-reduced version simultaneously. If you don't, by the time you get around to engineering the cost-reduced version, your competitor will have done it for you! Advanced technology is spread around in so many places that it's not possible for a company to control it all. You can't set the direction and, therefore, you can't really control your future. You have to give up on that concept, and you must go into the market knowing that other companies' technological advancements are setting the route for you.

The Electronic Elite know that their current product is destined to be replaced, either by a product of their own or by a product from a competitor. What's more, they realize that the new product may be very different from their current product. It may use a totally different technology, or it may be sold and marketed a completely different way. The Electronic Elite, when they see the market about to shift, are not afraid to sacrifice their old products in favor of new ones. To the contrary, often they replace their current products long before the market knows that it "needs" a new generation.

Beale/Financial Times/London

Reprinted by permission of Roger
Beale. Copyright © 1993 by Roger
Beale.

This attitude differs significantly from that found among traditional computer vendors who, like many other companies, tend to
be terrified of abandoning a currently profitable product in favor
of something new. That's exactly what happened at Digital in the
1980s. It was more concerned with protecting the market territory
it had already captured than with entering into new businesses, especially those that might threaten its current revenue.

Throughout the 1980s, it was clear to most people in the computer industry that the personal computer would eventually be capable of performing the computing tasks that were currently being
implemented on minicomputers and mainframes. The personal
computer represented the new generation of computing. Novell

fully understood this and decided to concentrate on building networks for this new generation of computers.

STRATEGY 3: BUILD SYMBIOTIC RELATIONSHIPS

Symbiosis, a concept that the Electronic Elite have borrowed
from ecology, is the process by which two or more organisms of
different species cooperate to enhance their ability to survive. In
an ecosystem, symbiotic relationships often develop between
species that might normally be enemies. For example, there's a
variety of bird in Florida that forages for food in the open
mouths of alligators. The alligators get their teeth cleaned and
the birds get a free lunch. The two exist in a state of symbiosis,
providing mutual benefit.

Most traditional organizations treat relationships as a zero-sum
game, where there are always winners and losers, just as there would
be on a battlefield. The notion of mutualism or symbiosis is never
considered. That's why so many traditional companies try to capture
all the profit. The motto of the Industrial Age manager is "never
leave money on the table." In this game, the winner is the company or
person who extracts the most profit from every situation. This attitude precludes different companies from working together because
somebody has to lose in order for somebody else to win.

The concept of symbiosis, by contrast, permits more complex
relationships between organizations. One of the major reasons
that Novell was able to grow a profitable networking business was
that it developed symbiotic relationships with the small, independent dealers that sold and installed Novell's software. This
arrangement allowed Novell to concentrate on what it did best—
building great software—and let the independent dealers concentrate on what they do best—remaining close to the customer and
providing the service needed to make the networks run smoothly.
Novell and the independent dealerships created a state of symbiosis that's been profitable for both.

The Electronic Elite are always searching for win-win symbiotic situations. This permeates their business deals, their attitude

toward their employees, and even, to a certain extent, their relationships with their competitors. Electronic Elite companies often
find it profitable to partner *and compete* with the same companies.
This phenomenon is so common that a new word has been coined to
describe this business behavior: *co-opetition.*

Let me give you an example of how this works. Microsoft
sells the popular Windows operating system software that runs on
IBM-style personal computers. The main competition for the Win-
dows/IBM PC combination is Apple's Macintosh personal computer. Apple and Microsoft are continually vying for market
share, a competition that has been going on for many years. But
Microsoft and Apple aren't just competitors, they're also business
partners. How can this be? Microsoft also sells the most popular
word processor and spreadsheet programs for the Macintosh, so obviously, without Microsoft, fewer people would be buying a Macintosh; and without Apple, Microsoft would lose part of its highly
profitable applications software business. The two companies are
involved in co-opetition—competing in one realm and cooperating
in another. This would be impossible if Microsoft and Apple viewed
each other as implacable enemies. Apple and Microsoft executives
can't afford to take this narrow, militaristic view of the situation.
The ecosystem mindset allows them to be more flexible in their
approach.

Electronic Elite companies aren't obsessed with the idea of destroying the competition. Their primary competitive motivation
is positive—they want to grow a business and increase the overall
size of the market. Sometimes, they even cooperate with companies in the same marketplace to "heat up" the market—so that
everyone makes more money.

One member of the Electronic Elite who understands this is
Sally Narodick, the CEO of Edmark, a Seattle-based company
that develops and publishes educational software and print materials for early childhood and special education students. This is a
company with a mission. According to their four-page personnel
policy manual, their purpose is "to provide high-quality educational products that enhance children's potential by combining

the power and the wonder of technology with proven educational content and instructional design." Sally gave up a powerful position in a bank to follow her dream of starting a software company. I could hear the ecological thinking (along with a good deal of playfulness) when Sally talked about the way her company approaches business:

> We're in a ballgame, and we get to play in a ballgame that is in this rapid growth phase. Here is the game plan: We've got to do extremely well, clear as a bell in front of everybody, and we celebrate our successes on that. And our game plan is to carve a very different niche and position for our products relative to the competitors.

Sally uses the ecosystem mindset to visualize a niche where her company can grow and prosper, which frees her company from the shackles of win-lose and zero-sum.

The Electronic Elite use the ecosystem mindset to provide the groundwork for symbiotic relationships that strengthen their companies' positions and help to grow the demand for innovative products. Is it any wonder the Electronic Elite also find it so easy to outmaneuver, outdevelop, and outsell the overregimented behemoths of the past?

For the Electronic Elite, the ecological mindset provides valuable insights into what really works in the Information Age. Companies that embrace this mindset find it easier to remain flexible, grow new businesses, and establish positive business relationships. Companies that remain tied to the Business=Battlefield mindset are naturally and inevitably led toward strategies that were more appropriate for the slow market cycles of the Industrial Age. This difference is shown in Figure 2.2.

POINTS TO PONDER

Keeping Figure 2.2 in mind, consider the following questions, which will help you personalize what has been discussed so far. Some of the questions are deliberately open-ended. The intent is to get you to imagine how you can deal with the challenges that

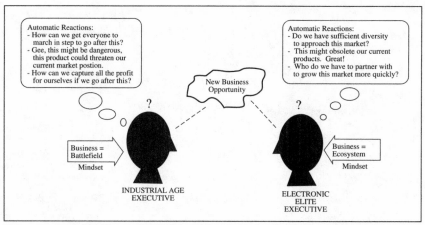

FIGURE 2.2. *Different Corporate Cultures Drive Different Business Strategies*

your organization is likely to encounter in the exciting years ahead.

- Is there a lot of tough, macho talk in your organization? What might be the consequences of that kind of thinking? Has this corporate militarism been a help or a hindrance in your current marketplace?
- Is there diversity of background and opinion in the top management of your company? In the rest of the company's management? What kind of "new blood" would make your organization more diverse and therefore more adaptable? And how would you make such a change possible?
- How would your organization react if your current products or services were suddenly made obsolete by new technology? Would it be able to move into new markets? Would it be willing to make its own products or services obsolete?
- Who are your organization's partners? Who wins when you win and vice versa? Is your organization trying to do everything itself? Could you be making more money if you formed symbiotic relationships with your customers? With your competitors?

Chapter Three

The Corporation Is
a Community

Everyone knows that Microsoft has made millionaires of hundreds of its employees. Less commonly known is that many of these millionaires continue to work at Microsoft after they've achieved financial independence. That probably sounds crazy to you, especially if you're one of those who insists "If I win the lottery, the first thing I'll do is tell my boss to take this job and shove it." Certainly, for most people, becoming wealthy would be a ticket to quit. But evidently some of the Microsoft millionaires don't see it that way.

This phenomenon of the devoted Microsoft employee is more exceptional when you consider that Microsoft working conditions aren't easy. Sixty-hour workweeks aren't uncommon, and when there's a major product release, workweeks move into the triple digits. Microsoft isn't known for great employee perks, either; on the contrary, Microsoft is notoriously thrifty. For many years, Chairman Bill Gates drove himself to the airport and flew coach when on Microsoft business, according to a former Microsoft vice president.

So, what would cause a bunch of millionaires (not to mention a billionaire or two) to stick with such demanding jobs longer than was economically necessary? The answer is simple: it's the sense of community, of belonging to something greater than the self. Microsoft has a very deep sense of community. People there feel as if they belong to something special. Here's what Microsoft Chairman Bill Gates said about the culture he helped to create:

> Our corporate culture nurtures an atmosphere in which creative thinking thrives, and employees develop to the fullest potential. The way Microsoft is set up, you have all the incredible resources of a large company, yet you still have that dynamic small-group, small-company feeling where you can really make a difference. Individuals generate ideas, and Microsoft makes it possible for those ideas to become reality. Our strategy has always been to hire strong, creative employees, and delegate responsibility and resources to them so they can get the job done.

This sense of community is not unique to Microsoft. The rest of the Electronic Elite are obsessed with creating a similar sense of belonging in their organizations, which deepens the work experience and adds value to the lives of employees. One articulate spokesperson for the Corporation=Community mindset is Frank Ingari, CEO of Shiva. I asked him how companies like Shiva inspire the kind of loyalty that brings out the best in their employees. Frank told me:

> The need to collaborate with a group to create a product taps into something really deep in the human psyche. It might have something to do with the breakdown of the family. Today, you don't have the shared sense of life experience with family and community the way you once did. We're no longer a band of pioneers moving to America. Neither are we a band of farmers raising our children together in the fields of Sicily. We don't have that any more. We're all nuclear families, if we're even in families at all. Because we're so alone, there's something really deep that wants you to tap into a shared effort.

It's human nature to want to belong to something greater than the self. One of the most common ways to achieve this is to associate with people with whom you share a common interest. That's increasingly difficult in today's fragmented world, where families are constantly being uprooted and moved from place to place. Because ties to geographic communities have been weakened by our nomadic society, it's only natural that people should turn to the workplace to satisfy this important human need.

After talking to Frank, I was somewhat troubled. I wondered, were the Electronic Elite taking advantage of their employees, using the loneliness inherent in modern life as leverage to get people to work harder? To Frank, though, satisfying this need for connection is a vast improvement over the dehumanizing work environments so common in Industrial Age corporations. Frank commented:

> We provide people with the opportunity to experience the positive aspects of collaborative work. I really believe in trust and diversity and empowerment, and when to back off and when to press on. These things are really important in people's lives. After all, we spend more time with our colleagues than we do with our spouses.

To Frank, the Corporation=Community mindset is a matter of *satisfying* rather than *exploiting* a basic human need. The Electronic Elite want the individuals in their organizations to extract more than just money from their work experience. The Electronic Elite want people to enjoy what they're doing.

Don't misunderstand: The Electronic Elite don't encourage this sense of community as an act of altruism. On the contrary, this is a very practical matter. The nature of competition in the Information Age requires workers to spend long hours at work. The Electronic Elite know that people won't work as hard if they aren't enjoying themselves and attaining some personal as well as professional satisfaction. It's essential that they feel they are surrounded by people they trust and who share the same goals. In other words, sustained productivity is difficult unless employees feel that they're part of a community.

Few companies, however, can also be considered communities. Instead, many people in business today—executives and employees alike—are far more prone to think of their companies as gigantic machines, which is unfortunate, because the Corporation= Machine mindset has some seriously detrimental consequences.

THE TRADITIONAL MINDSET: CORPORATION=MACHINE

James Champy, in his 1995 book *Reengineering Management: The Mandate for New Leadership*, writes that one reason many companies have become uncompetitive is that "modern day management thinking" is based on the notion of the "corporate machine." Champy points out that economic conditions have made this view of the corporation an anachronism, and that the behaviors, such as the centralization of power that the metaphor encourages, now constitute a recipe for failure.

Despite this, the Corporation=Machine mindset is still popular. Listen to the way executives talk and business authors write about corporations. A successful corporation is often said to be a "well-run" or even a "well-oiled machine"; it also is said to be a "good system," one that is "efficient" and "well-designed." When you hear these descriptions or hundreds of others like them, you're hearing the Corporation=Machine mindset at work.

The Corporation=Machine notion implies that corporations can be improved by changing the "design" of their processes, just as you might rework the inner mechanism of a complicated machine. Ironically, the word "reengineering" can throw a mental roadblock right in front of any attempt to change a corporation. Machines are, by nature, rigid; a good machine is stable, orderly, and organized. Machines never grow; they never change on their own, except when they break down due to sheer age or improper care. When you want to change a machine, it has to be reengineered to do something different, which is, by definition, a long and costly process.

If you think of a corporation as a machine, then changing it is like taking a jackhammer to a steam engine. You might be able to create something useful out of the fragments, but it is unlikely. To the machine-minded executive, corporate change is always sacrificing something that works in favor of the unknown. How many corporate change efforts have been derailed by the cliché "If it ain't broke, don't fix it"? This might be good advice for an automobile mechanic, but it may not be the best way for corporations to adapt to new market conditions.

Furthermore, machines need to be "run." The Corporation= Machine mindset encourages top management to visualize themselves in the control room of a big machine. Executives who think this way inevitably find it difficult to let people make their own decisions. This mindset can make top management feel powerless as well. The CEO of Xerox once confessed to a friend of mine:

> I feel like the captain of an aircraft carrier. I turn the wheel and try to point the ship in a new direction, but I have no idea whether or not my orders are being followed.

Managers who think this way can't *lead* an organization because they're too busy trying to *run* it.

One of the most debilitating effects of the machine mindset is the way that it dehumanizes people. Nobody is essential; anybody can be replaced. What's important is the "system," the great machine, how well it's run, how well it's "engineered" or "reengineered." Naturally, any corporation where this mindset is rampant will not reward creative thinking or recognize the value of intellectual differences.

People who feel they're just part of a machine aren't going to go out of their way to help an organization achieve its goals. In the worst case, they might be tempted to exact some kind of revenge on the company that's treating its employees like subhumans. When organizations treat employees like cogs in a wheel, work slows to a crawl. People do the minimum, just enough to keep from getting fired.

In the Electronic Elite organization, the opposite is the case. Because the Electronic Elite think of themselves as leaders of a community, rather than controllers of a corporate machine, they find it easier to get people connected to the organization's larger goals. Table 3.1 identifies the differences between the two approaches.

TABLE 3.1. *Comparison of Machine and Community Mindsets*

CORPORATION = MACHINE	CORPORATION = COMMUNITY
Dehumanization. The system is more important than the individual. People are merely cogs in the corporate machine.	*Humanization.* The individual is more important than the system. People provide the creativity and drive that creates profit.
Elimination of Labor. The perfect corporation consists of a CEO pulling the levers in a factory that has no people, only machines.	*Career Development.* Education and training increase the value of the community to the marketplace.
Alienation. Employees feel disconnected to the goals of the organization and, therefore, do the absolute minimum required to "get by."	*Connection.* Employees develop a deep loyalty to the higher goals of the organization, and make an extra effort to turn the dream into a reality.

To understand the value of the Corporation=Community mindset, let's examine a story that's an archetype for the vast changes that the computer industry has undergone. It's a David versus Goliath story of how a wet-behind-the-ears college kid built a multibillion-dollar company that captured major market share away from one of the largest and most respected companies in the world. It's also a story about how a community can overcome a machine by keeping people in touch with the higher goals of the organization.

CASE STUDY: IBM AND DELL COMPETE IN THE PC MARKET

During the years the microprocessor was first being built into computers, Michael Dell was a teenager in Austin, Texas. Michael was interested in microprocessors and thought that there might be a business opportunity there. Nevertheless, this notion wasn't developed enough to keep him from seeking a college degree in a field that had little to do with computers or technology.

At the same time that Michael Dell was sifting through his freshman class schedule, a thousand miles away in Boca Raton, Florida, a new division of IBM had just been formed. This division was mandated to create an IBM product based on a microprocessor. This product came to be known as the IBM Personal Computer, the IBM PC.

IBM's PC division was not a typical IBM organization. It was heavy on engineers and light on the professional managers that ran the show at corporate headquarters. And it was no accident that the PC division was located in Boca Raton. The heads of this new division knew that if they were going to produce a product in record time, they had to be as far away as possible from the corporate bureaucrats and "quality police."

The IBM PC wasn't a typical IBM product, either. IBM's mainframes were made of hardware and software parts that had been constructed by IBM. The *proprietary* focus of IBM's mainframe and minicomputer design resulted in unique products that were difficult for a competitor to reproduce. This made a great deal of sense at the time of their development because it helped lock customers into using equipment from IBM—and *only* from IBM.

The PC, on the other hand, was constructed out of pieces and parts from other manufacturers. The central processing unit (CPU) chip—the brains of the computer—came from a little-known company called Intel. The operating system—the software that tells the CPU how to "think"—came from a backroom start-up by the name of Microsoft. This product "openness" meant that, unlike previous IBM products, the IBM PC could be *cloned* by other manufacturers. There was nothing to stop you or me from building an imitation IBM PC in our garages, a fact that was not lost on some future multimillionaires.

But constructing the IBM PC from spare parts not only was expedient (it sped up the development process), it also made good business sense. Even though competitors could imitate the IBM PC, IBM could set the standard; in fact, by keeping the PC open to imitation and competition, IBM helped ensure that it became the standard, giving IBM a favorable market position as the demand for personal computers grew. True, IBM would never be able to dominate the market for PCs as it had dominated the market for mainframes. But if IBM had not built an "open" machine, it would have had to design all the parts itself rather than purchase them from other manufacturers. This would have taken time that IBM didn't have. A long delay for an IBM entry into this market would have allowed Apple or some other competitor to capture so much of the market that IBM would have remained outside the market completely.

Eventually, a vast armada of IBM PCs captured the infant market. IBM's PC division was positioned perfectly to grow as the market grew. And grow it did. By 1987, the total sales of IBM PCs reached $6.5 billion, making IBM's PC division, by itself, nearly two-thirds as large as the second largest U.S. computer company at the time (Digital). IBM captured fully 25.5 percent of the personal computer market, dwarfing Apple, which was limping along with a meager 10.5 percent.

Then disaster struck. Don Estridge, the "father" of the IBM PC, was killed in a plane crash. It was Estridge who had helped convince IBM's top management to give the PC division the autonomy it needed to develop such an unconventional product in such a short amount of time. His death was an enormous blow to the morale of the PC division's employees who had worked so hard to make the PC a success. Further, it seemed to sound the death knell of the PC division's autonomy. The success of the PC inevitably caused IBM's bureaucrats to descend on the PC division like a plague of blue-suited locusts. The division's management was transported to New Jersey, where it would be closer to corporate headquarters, and subject to review and tighter supervision. The days of radical innovation were gone.

IBM's management tried to implement strategies that would have made sense 10 years before, but that were hopelessly obsolete in the world of the microprocessor. IBM assigned bureaucrats and quality engineers to oversee the follow-on product, the IBM PC-AT. It was 18 months late and flawed by a brittle hard drive that had a tendency to break unexpectedly, losing all the customer's data. Next IBM tried to put a stranglehold on the growing market by creating a proprietary standard for plug-in boards to augment the capabilities of PCs. But the other PC manufacturers refused to cooperate, further eroding IBM's leadership position as the pacesetter for PC design and implementation.

These blunders might not have proven so serious had IBM's mainframe group not seemed determined to make life difficult for the PC division. Rather than accepting the inevitable—that the microprocessor meant the end of the mainframe—IBM's mainframe proponents were determined to protect their turf, even if it meant that IBM's PC business would suffer. In effect, the mainframe group waged a war of silence against the PC, refusing to admit that the new device was making their mainframes obsolete. One former IBM vice president told me:

> When I worked in IBM's mainframe business, I used to say that by the time the mainframe guys figure out that we're in trouble, it'll be too late. That was in 1987. What surprised me was the rapidity with which the decline came. The whole thing fell apart in months, where normally you would expect that kind of decline to take some number of years. There were a lot of people in the ranks who were predicting it, and there were a lot of people at the very top who understood that it was inevitable as well. So what was the problem? It was this big bubble of upper and middle management. Akers [then CEO] couldn't do anything about it because he became the leader of that pack, partly by working with them. They were his friends; he grew up with them in the company, in the culture. So when it came time to do hard things—like canceling projects and firing people—he found it too difficult. IBM was full of very highly educated overachievers who made it to high levels. Nevertheless, the company became dysfunctional, so dysfunctional that it became difficult to change.

Meanwhile, back in Austin, Michael Dell was splitting his energies between his freshman classes and "wondering what to do on the weekends." Almost as an afterthought, he began selling add-on chips and disk drives that worked with IBM's PCs and the many compatible brands that were becoming available at the time.

Michael obtained these components from the same companies that supplied IBM; however, because Michael had virtually no overhead, he could sell them much more cheaply by mail than IBM could sell them through direct sales representatives. By 1984, his dorm-room business was grossing $80,000 a month. Michael branched into full-blown IBM-compatible PCs, selling them through the mail at a 40 percent discount over IBM's prices. The fledgling Dell Computer began to grow swiftly, often selling to the very customers that IBM was neglecting. Ten years later, Dell Computer was the fifth largest manufacturer of personal computer systems. IBM, on the other hand, had tumbled to number four, squandering its original 25.5 percent market share into a pitiful 8.5 percent share.

IBM once had a truly great PC division, as creative and innovative as any company in the computer business today, which it ruined with micromanagement and bureaucracy. Conversely, Dell Computer has grown to be a large company, but without the bureaucracy normally associated with a large company.

We could write off the success of Dell Computer as a fluke, but the Dell story is not unique. The computer industry is full of upstart companies that have trounced massively entrenched competition. For example, few people, even inside the computer industry, had ever heard of Microsoft before the personal computer exploded onto the scene. Add to that, companies such as COMPAQ, Gateway, Packard Bell, Acer, the list goes on . . .

There are many reasons that Dell Computer and the rest of the PC companies were able to steal market share away from IBM. One was that Dell had lower overhead and thus could sell computers at a lower price. But that's only the veneer atop the real story. Dell Computer had lower overhead because its employees were more productive than those at IBM. Why? One reason was that CEO Michael Dell believed in the value of a sense of community in his organization.

At 30, Michael Dell is one of the most successful entrepreneurs of his generation. Boyish and irrepressible, he brings enthusiasm to the job of running a Fortune 500 company. Michael reiterated the importance of community in the success of his company:

People look to the company as a place where they want to build a career and a life, and not as a place where you come for a little while, then leave and go somewhere else. We definitely want to build that sense of belonging and being a part of something. And, with a company like this, that's growing rapidly, there's every opportunity to do that, and I think you'd be really foolish not to take advantage of that kind of enthusiasm and excitement in the people who are building what we expect will be a great company.

IBM destroyed the feeling of community that had been forged at the Boca Raton plant; its top management believed that to make the PC division more productive they had to integrate it into the larger corporate machine. At IBM, the vision of the corporate machine made IBM blind to the reality that it's people who make products successful, not a system. A former IBM top executive told me:

I've spent 13 years of my life inside large public institutions like IBM, where an individual doesn't really matter. You quit, they replace you. You move from job to job. You're an interchangeable part. It's left over from the Industrial Age, and it's wrong, and I hate it. It takes the value out of the individual. It's people who actually make these institutions work, not the system. There are people who want to blame the system for making people dispensable. It gives management a safer, more secure feeling. Somebody quits, no problem, we'll replace him. It's a socialist view of the world, and it's ridiculous. The individual is very important to success. Every interesting company and every interesting product is the creation of a few individuals. Period.

The Electronic Elite reject the mechanistic notion of the corporation; for them, the corporation is a community, and they take a lot of pride in the communities that they create. Mitchell Kertzman, CEO of Powersoft, commented:

One of the great satisfactions of having built this company is having something that I started myself. Now that we employ hundreds of people, we have social events, we see all the families and the children. There are a lot of human beings involved in this enterprise, and they're of tremendously high quality; they're fanatically committed to Powersoft, and they really believe in what they're doing. It's an amazing thing to have helped to put together something that people can feel so strongly and positively about.

The Electronic Elite use three specific strategies to build a feeling of community inside their organizations:

- Communicate directly.
- Create opportunities for social interaction.
- Make work fun.

Let's look at each of these in more detail.

Strategy 4: Communicate Directly

In general, it's easier for small corporations to maintain a sense of community than large corporations. When all the people in an organization work together intimately on a daily basis, they're forced to communicate with one another, and a sense of community arises naturally. There's a feeling of shared goals and shared responsibilities. When people talk, they form social bonds; that's human nature. Communicating brings people together.

That process is more difficult in large organizations. People begin to lose track of who has joined the organization. Some move to remote facilities, making one-on-one communication difficult. If the organization isn't careful, growth may result in a loss of this all-important atmosphere. I asked Shiva CEO Frank Ingari how he would structure an organization so that it didn't sacrifice its community atmosphere:

> There's no cookbook answer to organization, and the needs change over time; and there are many ways to organize. I absolutely want to retain the feeling of connectedness—it's difficult, though. The notion of connectedness to the corporation becomes more tenuous, more communications-oriented than physical and literal. In other words, in a company like Lotus, you're connected to Lotus by what you read in the press and what your in-laws read in the press. You're connected to Lotus by its image in the community, by its benefits

package, and what your spouse thinks about how generous the benefits are. Those are very, very different things than being connected to Lotus because you got drunk with the CEO last night at the barbecue.

Organizations and the people who lead them thus have an ongoing challenge when it comes to maintaining community in the organization, but it can be maintained if management pays attention. A company like Hewlett-Packard (HP) is proof that a company can maintain a high level of connectedness, even as it grows.

The key, according to Lewis (Lew) Platt (chairman of the board, president, and chief executive officer of Hewlett-Packard Company) is to use every means possible to keep the feeling of connectedness alive. Lew joined HP in 1966, and he has held a plethora of corporate positions since that time. Lew is an intensely private man, and he rarely grants interviews, preferring to concentrate his energies on keeping HP from becoming complacent about its recent successes. Lew explained how he uses his role as CEO to create a sense of connectedness at HP:

I do a lot of traveling, close to two-thirds of my time, and I spend a lot of time in front of HP people. I do this in fairly informal ways—like wandering around one-on-one, just talking to people. Other times, it's what we call coffee talk—the coffee talk is pretty famous here at HP. We get everybody at the site together and have a half hour where we talk about what's going on in the company, what's important, what's ahead, and then take some questions from the audience. I usually tack a half hour or an hour at the end to do some mingling with the people. These things are very important.

Lew's coffee talks aren't just public relations exercises. He actually listens to his employees and tries to incorporate their ideas into HP's corporate strategy. Through listening to and communicating with as many employees as possible, Lew shows he cares, and that permeates the entire organization.

Community building shouldn't be limited to live appearances. Electronic mail enables an organization's leaders to connect without actually traversing geographic boundaries, and even people working in remote sites around the world can feel that they're part of a corporate community. Shiva CEO Frank Ingari commented:

> As a large company, you have to organize to maintain multiple levels of connectedness. Manzi [then CEO of Lotus] sends regular electronic mail to all his employees, you know. Somebody drafts those for him, but he crafts them himself. He edits them, and he's very concerned with what they say, and they come from his desk under his name. Gates does the same thing.

As computer technology becomes more sophisticated, there are ever more opportunities and methods by which to connect. For example, at Sun Microsystems, a manufacturer of computer workstations, managers can send an electronic mail message to employees that contains a video clip that can be displayed right on their desktop computer screens. This allows managers at Sun to communicate their energy and enthusiasm immediately and directly to the employees. Electronic mail can help turn even a gigantic organization into a cyberspace village, where people around the world participate in the decision-making process. Chapter 10 discusses how to use electronic mail to strengthen a healthy corporate culture.

STRATEGY 5: CREATE OPPORTUNITIES FOR SOCIAL INTERACTION

Direct and frequent communication, even when augmented by powerful electronic communication, is not, however, enough to maintain sense of community. The Electronic Elite also make certain that there's plenty of face-to-face contact. One of the most effective ways is to create occasions for social interaction. Venture capitalist Ann Winblad explained to me how Electronic Elite organizations make people feel that they are an important part of the larger organization:

> They have functions for the new recruits, functions for the first-year recruits, functions for all the summer workers, and functions for Christmas. You're made to feel part of a winning team. I think

that that prevents burnout. Work becomes a social experience as well as just a work experience, and I think that's driven from the top leadership. I think the companies that have the least amount of burnout have a team approach, which really makes everyone feel like they're not just a cog in the wheel.

As Ann pointed out, the Electronic Elite sponsor a lot of social mixers. These events are very different from the typical Industrial Age company picnic where executives often don't attend or make only a symbolic appearance.

The Electronic Elite sponsor monthly or even weekly get-to-gethers so that people can connect to the organization. All levels of management are included, and everyone is encouraged to mingle freely. Michael Dell, CEO of Dell Computers, explained how this works:

> Any kind of activity where you can get people together and communicate is very helpful for our business. You have to break down barriers and promote informal communication. You build friendships within the company, and people begin to understand that "those people aren't out to get me; we're all in this together."

These social mixers need not be formal. For example, I once worked at a software development organization that had a tradition called a Quality Assurance (QA) Meeting. This semi-official meeting was held every Friday night at a local Mexican restaurant. Everyone was welcome, including spouses, children, and even former employees. These QA Meetings brought people from different organizations together, mostly to talk business, but also to discuss *Star Trek*, surfing, gardening, and many things of genuine concern to the corporate community. There was a free flow of information between organizations, managers, and employees.

Many times, these discussions ended in a burst of inspiration, and it wasn't unusual for a group of programmers to return to the office and work until the wee hours implementing something exciting, so that they could impress their colleagues when they returned to work on Monday. These QA meetings cost the corporation nothing because people paid their own way. However, the meetings were, at least in part, responsible for a rate of productivity in that group that was twice the industry average.

Integrating families into the workplace is another way to foster social interaction. If the corporate community is to replace the more traditional forms of community, then it *must* include families. One member of the Electronic Elite who has come to this conclusion is Bill Gross, the CEO of Knowledge Adventure, a developer of multimedia software for children. Bill used to work at Lotus where he had a broad range of product development responsibilities. As a result, Knowledge Adventure has become a pioneer in the inclusion of families as part of the corporate community. Bill commented:

> We integrate family life into the work environment in a variety of ways. I still try to do as much work as I can from home so I can be with my family. We also have a pretty open policy about staff bringing their families into the office, either after school or on weekends. A lot of us work on weekends, when there are a lot of kids around here playing. It's almost like a playroom for the kids, and they play with our products. We do of course have other things besides computers for them to play with—building blocks, coloring books, Legos, and all that. Having the kids around while we work has been great. We can go out to lunch together, the kids get to know each other, the parents get to spend time with their kids, and the parents get to show their kids what they do for a living. I'm really proud that I can show David what we're doing here; and the other kids, I think, are very proud of what their parents do.

Before the Industrial Revolution, men worked where they lived, on the farm and in craft workshops. This meant that fathers participated regularly in the raising and teaching of the children, and were more deeply integrated in the family and community life than is generally possible in an industrialized society. Today, as more and more women enter the workforce, there's a real danger that they too will become as alienated from their families as men have been.

According to Kristin Lund, vice president of the Illinois-based Praise and Leadership Schools, Inc. (a company that consults with corporations on in-house preschool programs), numerous studies have shown that business productivity is greatly improved by the presence of on-site child care. There is less absenteeism, decreased tardiness, less turnover, and increased job satisfaction. It also makes it easier for parents to remain in the workforce without sacrificing frequent day-to-day contact with their children.

It's important to include children as part of the corporate community. That's why it's exciting to see companies like Knowledge Adventure where children are a welcome part of the environment. Far from making organizations less productive, this policy is likely to make people more dedicated to the success of the corporate community.

Another good way to promote social interaction is sponsoring hands-on charitable events. Charitable contributions have always been part of the corporate scene, but the Electronic Elite tend to prefer small charities because they lend themselves to group activities, such as bake sales, benefit concerts, and the like, which build a sense of community. Michael Dell, CEO of Dell Computers, commented:

> One thing I think has worked particularly well for Dell in Austin is that our workforce is very active in volunteer and community activities. We regularly sponsor volunteer fairs, and the company, through its charitable donations, directs funds at those activities that employees participate in as volunteers. We poll our employees to understand what they're interested in and direct our funds toward those charities.

This kind of charitable contribution connects people not just to the organization, but to the community at large. Powersoft is a good example of this, according to CEO Mitchell Kertzman:

> I grew up in the 1960s, so I'm an old left winger, but I'm not as liberal as I used to be. However, the notion that we should build businesses that are culturally positive is a great thing. It also means the opportunity to be charitable. My company's very involved in education. For example, we partnered with a middle school in a depressed neighborhood nearby. We helped the students set up their

own business selling T-shirts so first they could learn leadership, entrepreneurship, and business skills. I like being a good corporate citizen, a good member of the community.

However, the Electronic Elite companies aren't charitable institutions. They are very serious for-profit companies, with difficult challenges in a highly competitive market. One of the fiercest competitors in the computer industry is Sun Microsystems, a manufacturer of high-powered workstations. According to *Fortune*, Sun is "the most efficient company in the industry," and *Business Week* praised 39-year-old CEO Scott McNealy as "making Sun Microsystems the model for the entire industry, including IBM." He says a big part of Sun's culture is its feeling of community:

> There's no company I know of that does more hours of volunteer work than this group. It's a community. The communication brings the community. Community has "comm" in it, as does communication. They're really the same words: community and communication. But it's really important to keep focused on the fact that if you don't make money, you lose the pride, you lose the funding, you lose the lifeblood of the organization. We're a community, but we're definitely not a nonprofit organization.

STRATEGY 6: MAKE WORK FUN

So far, we've looked at how Electronic Elite companies use direct communications and social interaction to create a feeling of community. But there's another element to community building that's very much a part of the world of the Electronic Elite—a sense of fun.

One company that carries this sense of fun to a delightful extreme is Sun Microsystems. In addition to Sun's sponsorship of sports activities, Sun has a tradition of April Fool's jokes, generally played by employees on their managers. For example, one manager at Sun discovered a replica of his office submerged in the bottom of an aquarium full of sharks. One of the cofounders, Bill Joy, found his Ferrari parked in a shallow pond, replete with a bumper sticker reading "I brake for flamingos." Even CEO Scott

McNealy isn't sacrosanct. He arrived one April Fool's morning to discover that his office had been turned into a one-hole, par-four miniature golf course.

What's important here isn't the silliness of the pranks, but the underlying cultural values that make these pranks acceptable. Because Electronic Elite organizations truly believe that work is supposed to be fun, they find occasions to make it so. It's also significant that the executives are the butt of the jokes. Can you imagine Andrew Carnegie, or General Electric CEO Jack Welsh for that matter, thinking it was not only funny, but appropriate, for their employees to turn a CEO's personal office into a golf course?

Many of the Electronic Elite treat their work as if it were their favorite hobby. Some employees come into work on weekends because they truly enjoy their jobs. Although there are exceptions, by and large, the employees of Electronic Elite companies look on work as one of the chief pleasures in their lives.

One company that encourages and expects its employees to treat work as their hobby is Microsoft. To learn about this, and other aspects of Microsoft's culture, I interviewed Mike Maples, who retired from Microsoft in mid-1995 after serving as executive vice president for worldwide products since 1988. Rotund and impressive, at 52, Mike was one of Microsoft's oldest executives, who also spent 23 years at IBM before joining Microsoft. I spoke to Mike right before he left the company, and he commented on how he and other Microsoft employees view their jobs:

> I'm really lucky that my job and that my hobby are the same thing. I go home on Saturday afternoons and the thing I want to do is play with software, look at it, see what other people have done and how they've done it, and how it might be useful. If I was working at a bank, I'd probably go home and work on computers on the weekend and in the evenings. We probably all share a passion for the technology and the products, which makes some of the outside activities kind of blend together. One of the things that I enjoy reading is computer books, and so, instead of reading about deer hunting, I'm reading about computers.

To be sure, these people work hard—very hard—but they bring a sense of joy to what they do. Take, for example, Edward McCracken, the CEO of Silicon Graphics Incorporated (SGI). SGI is the company that makes the high-powered workstations that Hollywood uses to create magic on the big screen, such as the dinosaurs that prowled through *Jurassic Park*. The market for this kind of high-tech computer is fiercely competitive, but Silicon Graphics, with over $1 billion in yearly revenues, has managed to stay on top, outpacing offerings from Digital, IBM, and a host of others.

Edward McCracken, a former executive from Hewlett-Packard, feels right at home in SGI's easygoing but intense corporate culture. With washed-out blond hair and piercing blue eyes hidden behind aviator glasses, he looks a little like a grown-up, hyperbrilliant version of the boy next door. He told me:

> We thrive on self-motivation. Our people work really hard and they play really hard. We think it's important that our people have fun working. We like to say that we have serious fun, because we produce what we think are the world's best systems. Our employees really relate to that.

Another high-morale environment is Powersoft, where CEO Mitchell Kertzman instituted a friendly competition called the Powersoft Award to reinforce the sense of playful community inside his organization:

> We recently instituted something called the Powersoft Award. We took nominations from employees for people they believe most epitomize the values of Powersoft. What's interesting about this is that we didn't specify what those values are. We didn't give them a lot of talk about courage and honesty and customer services. We just said that we felt that there was a common understanding of Powersoft's values. We had an anonymous committee of employees judge the nominations. The level of intensity and emotion in that room the day we announced the names was incredible. The reaction and response to the people who won was a validation that the choices had been right. These people were universally respected and admired and loved by their colleagues. There was no disagreement, no doubt that these people absolutely represented the best

values of the company: they had uncomplaining team spirit, willingness to help others, commitment to equality. It was sort of like when people say: "I don't know a lot about art, but I know what I like." We don't know what a Powersoft person is, but we recognize one when we see one, and one of the ways to perpetuate that is to find the best and hold them up as examples.

The idea that a corporation should expend resources making work fun is an almost unthinkable concept if you believe that a corporation is a machine. Who bothers to entertain a machine? Why would a cog want to laugh? And yet, if you replace the Corporation=Machine mindset with the Corporation=Community mindset, the idea of making work fun becomes not only logical but essential. Community building can't just be a way for the corporate machine to eke some extra labor out of the workforce. Community building, when approached the way the Electronic Elite recommend, is a part of a cultural revolution that values individuals and their contribution to the organization. Powersoft CEO Mitchell Kertzman commented:

I care a lot about the people here. It's more than just providing a flexible environment and good benefits and all those things. I try to create an environment where people can adhere to their personal high values and feel that these are consistent with the company's values and the company's goals. I believe that virtually every person knows the right thing to do in any situation. I want to create a company where that right thing to do by your value judgment as a good human being is also the right thing to do for the company. The right thing to do and what the company wants me to do should be congruent. They should be the same.

POINTS TO PONDER

The Electronic Elite use the sense of community to create organizations where people work hard, not because they feel that they'll be fired if they don't, not because they need the extra money to put food on the table, but because they feel like they're contributing to something special. This is possible only if the workplace satisfies the human need to participate in something greater than the self. The Electronic Elite, by changing the definition of corporation, reap the extraordinary profits that come from the dedication and loyalty of people who feel that they *belong*.

Keeping this in mind, here are some questions to help you integrate the issues raised in this chapter, and then incorporate them in your own organization:

- How often does your management communicate directly with employees? Are those communications truly informative or merely an opportunity to spout the company line? What could you do to promote a greater level of connection between your organization's leadership and the people who are actually making products, providing services, or serving customers?
- What kind of electronic communications facilities do you currently have (such as fax, e-mail, video conferencing)? Can these facilities be used to communicate with everyone or just a privileged few? What could you do today to promote a deeper level of electronic communications in your organization?
- Do you have a company picnic every year? Do the executives and their families attend and mingle with everyone else? What kind of company event could you recommend that wouldn't cost much, could be held frequently, and could bring people closer together?
- What would it take to start an in-house day care center or preschool at your corporation? What kind of priorities would the management have to adopt in order to make this a reality?
- Is there a way that you could make charitable giving something that would help to bind your organization together? What act of kindness or concern could your organization sponsor that would really make a positive difference to your local community?

Chapter Four

Management Is Service

Who isn't familiar with Bill Gates, the wunderkind who cofounded Microsoft and today is one of the richest men in the world? Bill is often in the news, and nearly every action that he and his company take is dissected in the business press. One of the reasons that Bill remains so fascinating is that he's very different from the CEOs of the past. For example, he's often seen wearing the sneakers and sport coats that engineers tend to favor, even though his wealth could obviously purchase Armani suits. But it isn't Bill's appearance that makes him such an interesting character. It's the way that he fills the role of Chairman at Microsoft.

As already noted, most CEOs think of themselves as "running" their companies. They consider themselves "captains of industry" with minions at their beck and call. Not so Bill. The last thing that Bill wants to do is to tell employees exactly what to do. He has no need to control the behavior of his employees; instead he wants to provide them an environment where they can accomplish their and the company's goals. Here's what Bill told me about his role at Microsoft:

> At Microsoft, the role of management is to spot emerging trends and set the future direction of the company. The most important and exciting part of my work as Chairman is recognizing what we

call "sea changes," and articulating the opportunities they present to each person in the company. We then empower employees with as much information and as many productivity tools as possible, so they can achieve results within the framework of that vision. The hardest part is knowing how to allocate the right resources—bet the store when we must—to make sure it all happens.

Bill is providing a service for the rest of Microsoft. It's his goal to *lead* Microsoft, rather than *run* Microsoft.

The rest of the Electronic Elite are as service oriented as Bill Gates. For example, I asked Edward McCracken, CEO of Silicon Graphics, how his company has continued to achieve success in such a highly competitive market. He told me that the key to innovation at Silicon Graphics is a lack of formal structure:

The good companies in the computer industry have horizontal organizations; they aren't as hierarchical, and people develop informal project teams with people on the Net. Communications are much easier, and more people know what's going on. And that's important, because if you're going to make quick decisions and get on with things that are changing so fast, you want each individual to be able to make informed decisions. We thrive on self-motivation.

McCracken manages SGI by giving self-motivated individuals the power to make their own decisions. As a result, there's a lot of freedom at SGI and not much bureaucracy. Although SGI, with over 5,000 people, is more than large enough by Industrial Age standards to justify a fairly extensive bureaucracy, it has never developed a significant bureaucracy. Instead, like most other Electronic Elite companies, it has developed a different way of thinking about the process of management. Rather than focusing on controlling employee behavior, Electronic Elite management tries to eliminate control mechanisms and disperse power throughout the organization.

To the Electronic Elite, as just explained, management isn't about control at all; it's about service. This is a difficult concept for many to grasp. We're used to thinking about managers, especially top executives, as people who tell other people what to do.

Another reason that the Management=Service mindset seems so foreign is that historically, service has been associated with a low-paying, often subservient, job. When we hear about the growth of the service economy, we tend to think of people flipping burgers or providing maid service. The notion that a multibillionaire such as Bill Gates provides a service to his own company initially sounds backward.

The Electronic Elite encourage and inspire; they help people to envision what the organization and they as individuals are capable of achieving. They also arbitrate when employees can't come to a decision on their own. On rare occasions, they will intervene and reverse decisions when they feel the organization, for one reason or another, goes off course. This, however, is the exception and not the rule. The Electronic Elite would rather that their organizations run smoothly and profitably without much management attention. Often, the Electronic Elite view having to intervene in day-to-day decision making as a failure on their part. This is a different attitude from that of the typical corporation, where management meddling is often ubiquitous.

THE TRADITIONAL MINDSET: MANAGEMENT=CONTROL

The idea that the role of management is to control employee behavior emerges naturally from the Business=Battlefield and Corporation=Machine mindsets. Managers who have internalized those two mindsets naturally conclude that they should be in "command" of the troops, and "controlling" the machine.

A major problem with the Management=Control mindset is that it leads corporations to concentrate power at the top. It causes the proliferation of complicated rules and regulations, the growth of bureaucracies, and the need for expensive reporting mechanisms to pass information up and down the management chain. Traditional companies believe that the result of such techniques will be a stronger, in-control corporation. Unfortunately, the actual result is likely to be a brittle and rigid monolith.

One victim of this mindset was Wang Laboratories in the 1980s. Wang was the leading vendor of stand-alone word processors, the special-purpose computers that assistants used to type memos for their bosses. By the mid-1980s, it was pretty clear that low-cost personal computers would replace Wang's pricey word processors as the platform of choice for word processing. This represented a wonderful opportunity for Wang Laboratories, because the software on Wang's word processors was the best and most sophisticated in the world. All Wang had to do was to convert its own word processing software to run on the personal computer, and it would probably have captured the soon-to-be-lucrative market for PC-based word processing software.

Wang didn't do this, however. The management knew that once Wang's leading-edge word processing software was on the personal computer, few people would be willing to buy Wang's word processor units. What Wang failed to realize was that it was only a matter of time before somebody else came up with a workable word processing program for the personal computer. When that happened, Wang's profitability quickly declined.

Wang's decision not to make the transition into PC-based word processing was a direct result of the company's culture, according to a former Wang executive:

> The organizational structure was extremely rigid. There were seven levels of management between the average product manager and CEO Wang. It's no wonder that he lost track of what was going on inside the company. By 1986, it was clear that personal computers would have a big impact on computing. Despite this, companies like Wang had great difficulty assimilating that fact.

Wang's problem was that the mechanisms of command and control, rather than making the company stronger, merely made it awkward and unwieldy.

The Management=Control mindset can also create a supercharged political atmosphere that saps the energy of the corporation with turf battles, labor unrest, power plays, and all the other futile behaviors that do absolutely nothing to serve customers.

The result is often a state of "control gridlock" where even the most basic of tasks—like bringing a product to market—becomes an extraordinarily complicated process involving many signatures, multiple approvals and agreements, and political gyrations.

A good example of this problem is Xerox, a company that's had a great deal of trouble getting products out the door. Here's what a former employee told me about working in a marketing group at Xerox:

> It was incredible. Everything, from the press release to the product description to the information sheet had to be reviewed and approved by multiple vice presidents and announcement committees. We spent almost six months trudging through the paperwork. If one committee or VP made a change to a paragraph, the other committees and VPs had to approve it. Even with electronic mail, it was an unbelievable hassle. Everything had to comply with corporate standards, even though some of the standards were inconsistent and often out-of-date. What was sad about the situation is that all these people sincerely believed that they were helping the company to be successful. There was no conception whatsoever that all this folderol was one of the reasons that Xerox was losing market share. They didn't have a clue.

We've been told for so many years that managers are supposed to be in charge that any other definition of management seems absurd or naive. All too often, well-meaning managers try to control their way out of problems, control the behavior of the people who work with them, control events that are going to happen whether they like it or not.

It's a popular business myth that large organizations need more control than smaller ones; in other words, the bigger the company, the bigger the bureaucracy. But even small organizations can be crippled by managers who believe that their position is dependent on trying to control events and employee behavior. Companies like Microsoft and Hewlett-Packard make it abundantly clear that organizations can be large and remain flexible.

A friend of mine, a marketing specialist, was once hired by an eight-person software start-up. He had spent the preceding few years at a large company (it was one of the minicomputer vendors) and was relieved to have the chance to work for a small company that presumably would be free of the political infighting and bureaucracy that had made his last job so miserable. When he arrived at his new job, the marketing vice president called him into her office and informed him that she didn't want him to speak directly to the company's president. If he had any comments or complaints, he was to talk to her first. "We've got to maintain discipline and order," she told him. At first he thought that she was joking—after all, there were only eight people in the entire company—but the rigid expression on her face told him that she was deadly serious. Not surprisingly, the company quickly ran into major problems and was nearly forced out of business.

The need to control can be very seductive. The illusion that we can bend other people's hearts and minds and get them to do exactly what we want is a comforting one in a world that's admittedly chaotic. What's most dangerous about "control" is that it works—at least for a while, but it eventually creates massive resentment. The controlling person looks around the conference table one day and finds that he or she is surrounded by enemies—people who would stab the controlling manager in the back, if given half a chance. So the manager comes up with some new way to control or manipulate, while the employees continue to maneuver and posture to avoid the heavy hand of management.

What's the alternative to control? Chaos? That's what best-selling author and management consultant Tom Peters would have us believe. Peters wrote a book, *Thriving on Chaos*, encouraging managers to embrace chaos, to channel it, to make chaos an integral part of the organization. Industry savant and venture capitalist Ann Winblad commented:

> The software industry as a whole tends to be slightly managed chaos. It was a giant "group grope" in the late 1970s when this whole thing started. Because of the fast growth of new segments, that has not changed. It probably is a little bit more civilized working at a large software company like Oracle than at a start-up down the street, but only marginally. I mean, they might have fancier

TABLE 4.1. *Comparison of Control and Service Mindsets*

MANAGEMENT=CONTROL	MANAGEMENT=SERVICE
Gridlock. The attempt to control creates resistance and spawns other attempts to control, causing decision making to grind to a halt.	*Flexibility.* Important decisions are moved away from top management and closer to the customer, making the company more responsive.
Yes Man Syndrome. People agree with their managers even when there are better ideas and better ways to approach a situation.	*Creative Dissent.* Different opinions and ideas result in a variety of approaches and ways of accomplishing a task.
Limited Power. Control concentrated at the top limits the exercise of power to the executives, slowing corporate growth.	*Empowerment.* Dispersing control downward increases the amount of power in the organization, making it more viable.

buildings and a security system and name tags, but effectively, there are no rules.

Think about that: "Effectively, there are no rules." Among the Electronic Elite, the addiction to control has been replaced by a different understanding of what management is all about. Electronic Elite managers set the overall direction of the organization and then let the employees decide how they're going to go after those opportunities. This Management=Service mindset results in a very different set of behaviors from the Management= Control mindset, as shown in Table 4.1.

To illustrate how these two mindsets produce different business results, let's look at how Hewlett-Packard overtook Digital Equipment Corporation as the second largest computer company in the United States.

CASE STUDY: THE ORGANIZATIONAL STRUCTURES OF HEWLETT-PACKARD AND DIGITAL

Hewlett-Packard (HP) is unique among all the computer vendors that were part of the 1970s boom in that it has weathered the vast changes of the past 15 years without the layoffs, bankruptcies, and market share losses that have crippled many of the rest.

HP was founded in 1939 by Bill Hewlett and Dave Packard, two electrical engineers from Stanford University. They had some unusual ideas about how to lead their fledgling company, which were contrary to management theories of that time. The 1940s and 1950s were a time when management was considered a science, and business schools encouraged managers to run companies "by the numbers." Boiled down to its essence, this meant maximizing profit by paying employees as little as possible to do their jobs. This kind of management remains popular today, according to Rafael Aguayo in his 1990 book *Dr. Deming: The American Who Taught the Japanese about Quality.*

Bill Hewlett and Dave Packard believed that a corporation would be more productive if employees also benefited from the corporation's success. Further, they believed that workers deserved a stable environment, absent of the "hire-and-fire" turmoil common in the electronics industry of the time. They also considered a strong corporation to be like a community, and created a tradition of informality; from the start, they were "Bill" and "Dave" to their employees. Finally, HP's founders pointed employees in the right direction and let them do their jobs. Micromanagement had no place inside HP's corporate culture. Bill and Dave created a culture in which management was a service to the people doing the work. HP grew and prospered, and increasingly by the late 1970s, HP's revenues were coming from computer products such as the HP 3000 minicomputer.

One of HP's major competitors at this time was Massachusetts-based Digital Equipment Corporation. Digital was founded in 1957 by Ken Olsen, an electrical engineer from MIT. As Digital grew, Ken—a self-styled puritan who neither drank, smoked, or swore—centralized control of the company, purging anybody who represented a possible threat to his authority. This process, documented in Rifkin and Harrar's 1988 book *The Ultimate Entrepreneur: The Story of Ken Olsen and Digital Equipment Corporation,* resulted in a company that ran according to Ken's every whim. He even coined a corporate motto to epitomize his concept of Digital: "One Company, One Strategy, One Message." Ken's motto was symbolic of his determination to be an absolute monarch. It was the Management=Control mindset taken to an extreme. This attitude, and the resulting organizational structure, became a major weakness at Digital, according to Jim Manzi, then CEO of neighboring Lotus Development Corporation:

> One of the things that killed Digital was the "Ken Says" phenomenon. You know, unless "Ken said," nothing happened. It was a very Copernican world where everything revolved around Ken. That's true in all sorts of companies. But that's death in today's world.

By 1980, HP and Digital were similar on the surface, both selling minicomputers to the same kind of customers. Beneath the surface, however, things were very different. HP had a decentralized and flexible corporate culture that trusted employees to make decisions on their own. Digital, on the other hand, had a corporate culture that was permeated with control. At that time, Digital was the more successful; in fact, Digital was the world's largest minicomputer vendor and soon to become North America's second largest computer vendor (after IBM). By 1988, Digital was still in the lead, enjoying $12.4 billion in yearly revenues, a little less than twice HP's yearly computer revenues.

By 1994, the positions of the two companies had reversed. HP's yearly sales were up to $24 billion, and the company was growing at a breakneck 24 percent per year. Digital's revenues had stalled at $13.5 billion, less than they were in 1988 when adjusted for inflation. And worse, Digital's growth rate was a depressing 6.4 percent. HP was enjoying record profits, while Digital had recently experienced a series of record losses. Hewlett-Packard's CEO Lew Platt told me how HP accomplished this:

> Hewlett-Packard is very much managed by culture. A lot of thing around here just happen because that is the right way to do things at HP. We are a very decentralized company. We're broken down into relatively small business units. We give people who run the businesses a lot of freedom in terms of making decisions about

what they ought to be doing. We don't try to steer everything from the top of the company. I think that gives us the advantages of being big—and there are some—while it allows us to avoid most of the disadvantages.

According to Lew, being decentralized has kept HP closer to its customers. Because decisions are made closer to the customer, HP makes products that customers want. He believes that HP's decentralization is responsible for HP avoiding the arrogance and complacency that developed at IBM and Digital. He explained:

You can't start believing that you're invincible or that you know what customers want more than they do. That has been the Achilles' heel of many companies in this industry, particularly our two biggest competitors. They became complacent. And, when they became complacent, they decided that they knew what customers needed better than the customers knew. They stopped listening, and they started missing all the subtle signals in the marketplace that they would have picked up had they been more alert.

Decentralization helped HP to remain responsive to customer requirements. As a result, HP entered the personal computer market early. Today, HP's widely dispersed and decentralized divisions not only sell desktop computers, they produce a line of portable and ultrasmall computers. HP's printer division virtually dominates the market for desktop printers. And HP is one of the most innovative companies in the computer industry, leading the research and development for new technologies such as the superfast P7 microprocessor that HP and Intel are building together.

HP has successfully adapted to the new computer industry because its decentralized structure made it possible to create innovative products quickly. Not that it's been easy. The computer industry of the 1990s has changed radically from the computer industry of the 1970s. Like the other traditional computer vendors in the 1990s, HP has had to deal with lower margins, fiercer competition, and an ever-more-demanding customer base. What's interesting is the way that HP reacted to these major challenges. Rather than trying to consolidate control at the top as many companies would have done, HP reacted by decentralizing even further. CEO Lew Platt explained:

> If you study carefully the history of HP, you will find in every case—and I am more certain about this than anything else I've said to you today—when we've gotten into trouble, it has always—not almost always—it has *always* been followed by a period of decentralization and pushing decision making down. That's just the way we respond. And, again, it works. And because it works and because HP people tend to be around for a very long time, there are always a lot of people who remember the last time that it worked. Therefore, you have a large number of people who are willing to bet that it will work again. There's a quote that I particularly like: "The role of the CEO is to make the invisible visible and to manage the white spaces." That is a clever way of saying that the CEO is really responsible for the sense of connectedness within the company, the white spaces being those things between the functions or the businesses on the organization chart. I really like that definition of the CEO's job. I think that's what the CEO's job is all about, and I spend a lot of my time doing it.

By contrast, Digital's top-heavy structure made it difficult for the company to launch the products that customers wanted. Founder Ken Olsen didn't like personal computers and didn't see why people needed them. This prejudice was widespread at Digital's corporate headquarters, which held most of Digital's decision-making power. As a result, Digital didn't launch a viable personal computer business until 10 years after the IBM PC had been released.

Unlike HP, which decentralized further in response to financial problems, Digital, consistent with its Management=Control culture, increased the level of control when Digital's financial fortunes began to wane. Digital's management instituted top-down financial controls and strengthened the power of the internal bureaucracy. The board of directors hired "strong" managers from traditional companies such as IBM, hoping that they could "pull the company together." Then the layoffs started. In the first rounds, most of the people who were laid off were "in the field," far away from corporate headquarters. In essence, Digital purged the very people who were closest to the customers and might have been able to help Digital adapt to changing customer requirements. Not surprisingly, by May 1994, *Business Week* bemoaned that Digital was worse off than ever before. (Since then, Digital has been slowly trying to transform its culture, and the Digital of today is different from the one that blundered so badly in the past.)

This example shows that the Management=Service mindset supports three successful strategies that make organizations more responsive and adaptable:

- Increase power by dispersing it.
- Encourage creative dissent.
- Build autonomous teams.

Let's examine each of these strategies.

STRATEGY 7: INCREASE POWER BY DISPERSING IT

Traditional companies concentrate control at the top of the company through the formation of a powerful bureaucracy at corporate headquarters. At many companies, that bureaucracy can become, like government bureaucracy, an impediment to meaningful change. The Electronic Elite make a constant effort to avoid the bureaucratic encrustations that plague so many other companies. Hewlett-Packard CEO Lew Platt commented:

> I am convinced that bureaucracy and centralization tend to accumulate over time. I'm fond of drawing a parallel to what happens in your garage. Junk accumulates, and if you don't clean house periodically, you find you can't park your car! Bureaucracy is the same way. It's always creeping into the system, and periodically you have to stand back and really clean it out. We do that. We're reasonably good at doing that. We've taken things such as our corporate headquarters' functions and have an annual review of them.

The businesses get to vote on whether they want them to continue. That helps us clean out whatever bureaucracy has crept in.

At HP, you have a perfect example of the Industrial Age corporation set on its ear. In most companies, the various divisions have to go to corporate bureaucracies every year, begging for approval to continue their work. At HP, the situation is exactly reversed; the corporate functions have to go to the divisions for funding.

The Electronic Elite also keep power from accumulating at the top of the organization by making sure that they, as CEOs, don't cling to a need to tell people what to do. One CEO who has become a master of this is Mitchell Kertzman. I asked him the secret to becoming an effective manager. Here's what he told me:

I am the reverse of the Peter Principle. When I started the company, it was a one-man business. There was a time when I did every job in this company. I wrote the programs, I sent out the bills, I did the accounting, I answered the phone, I made the coffee. As the company has grown, I do fewer and fewer of those jobs. And that's just as well, because I was certainly less competent at them than most of the people who are doing them now. I'm the reverse of the Peter Principle in the sense that I've finally risen to my level of competence, which is that I don't do anything very well and now what I do extremely well is nothing. Now, what am I good at? I'm good at motivation. I'm good at recruiting. I'm good at representing the company. I'm good at giving speeches. I'm good at meeting with customers, meeting with the press, working with the financial community. So, my job has become what I'm good at.

For Mitchell, the process of growth as a manager was the process of giving up control, responsibility, and authority. The key to personal growth as a manager is to recognize your weaknesses and then overcome them by hiring great team members. Giving up control is different from delegating, according to Mitchell. As he explained it, managers who delegate are still tied up in the need to control:

The unwillingness to let go is almost a pathology. They know—intellectually—that they need to hire good people to do these things, but then they don't let go. Part of the problem is delegating. Delegating implies that the job is yours but you are delegating it to someone else to do in your place. That's different from saying, "I'm the CEO and the whole company's performance is my responsibility, but running operations belongs to Joe, and running finance belongs to Jane." It's my job to encourage them, provide them the resources that they need, support them, be critical.

As you can see, there's a definite "service" orientation to Mitchell's view of management. That doesn't mean that he lacks power. Because he's so respected, people listen to what he has to say, and ultimately, the decision-making power rests with him. However, to increase the overall power in the organization, he's chosen to disperse it, using it himself only rarely.

Management=Control also contributes to weak corporate structures by insisting that managers can, and should, know everything that's going on inside an organization. This is a big mistake, according to former Lotus CEO Jim Manzi:

Hierarchy and authority exist in people's minds and perspectives. My greatest fear is having people walk around this company saying, "Jim says we should do this" or "Jim says we do that." The truth is that Jim really doesn't know what these people are talking about because there is a ton of stuff going on in the company. My goal is to make sure that everybody's working in a common direction. I tell people that I don't know what they're talking about. I tell them to leave me out of it. I tell them this is not something I get involved in. I'm very explicit. I'm trying not to encourage the notion that I know everything that's going on in the company, which is a disease a lot of managers have.

The Electronic Elite relinquish control to make the entire organization more powerful. Frank Ingari, CEO of Shiva, commented on this seeming paradox:

Let me ask you something: Do you think power is finite, or do you think power is a renewable resource and, in fact, a global resource inside the company? What happens in the large company is that sooner or later people begin to believe that power and all the associated goodies—power for its own sake, power as an aphrodisiac, power as access to money, power as access to bosses—is a finite pool. For one person to have power, another has to lose it. Despite what people think, that's not true, even in a large company. In fact, it's a sign of impending death when people inside a company start believing that. Nothing could be further from the truth. Power doesn't derive from what happens inside these four walls. Power derives from our effect in the marketplace, and from what we're able to generate within ourselves in terms of creative activity. Therefore, by definition, the exact opposite is true. Power can and must be grown. The successful company is growing its power.

Therein lies the real meaning of the much-abused word "empowerment"—by giving up control, by empowering people in the organization, you make it more robust, more adaptable, more flexible, and, therefore, more powerful.

STRATEGY 8: ENCOURAGE CREATIVE DISSENT

Dispersing power into an organization won't work if managers, including CEOs, get into a huff every time somebody in the organization does something that management doesn't like. Managers can't constantly be intervening to make things the way they want it. This means they must tolerate and encourage dissent, even if that dissent is with the management itself. This strategy is illustrated by the following story that Mitchell Kertzman told me about the way he manages Powersoft:

A while back, a junior manager in the company came up with an idea that I thought was really dumb. And I made it very clear that I thought it was dumb. He went ahead and did it anyway. Well, I was wrong and he turned out to be exactly right. The important part, culturally, is that I should be able to stand up and acknowledge that I was wrong, and support a person who, in spite of my disagreement, went ahead and did what turned out to be the right thing.

Mitchell let the junior manager do what he thought was appropriate and Mitchell was willing to admit that he was wrong. This kind of event rarely, if ever, happens in an Industrial Age company because that junior manager would never have dared to disagree with his traditional CEO in the first place. And he undoubtedly would have been fired had he taken an action that was contrary to the CEO's opinions about the right way to do things, regardless of whether it worked or not.

For the Electronic Elite, the process of decision making is collaborative, with the manager playing a role as arbitrator, coach, and mentor rather than officer, owner, and dictator. This isn't to say that the Electronic Elite can't or won't make decisions. They do make final decisions, but generally only when employees can't come to agreement.

One particularly dynamic Electronic Elite leader is William Campbell, the CEO of Intuit, the company that makes the most popular personal finance software in the world. I spoke with Bill at his home in Silicon Valley and despite the relaxed surroundings, Bill frequently became passionate and excited about the ideas that he felt were important. Bill believes that controlling organizations strip away individual initiative. Employees metamorphose into "yes men" and corporate "fraidy cats," a problem he saw at IBM:

> IBM is like the Stepford Wives. It takes the best people from the best colleges and universities in the country and then snips out some part of the brain so that they become mindless clones. They're still, individually, some of the smartest people I know, and I really enjoy them when I get them in a bar. But inside of IBM, they don't protest, they don't fight anything, they're afraid to take risks. They're always talking about what *won't* fly in the company.

In his leadership role, Bill tries to set up a corporate environment where there's plenty of controversy, opinions, and conflict. He uses this as a way to get people involved in the decision-making process:

> You get used to working with equals. It makes you manage differently. The hierarchical manager of yesterday ran the Industrial Age company with "Yes sir! Yes sir! Anything you want, sir! I'm right with you sir!" Now it's all different. People talking to management

say things like, "Bill, that's bullshit. That's stupid. You made a dumb decision." That's the difference. When you're running an Information Age company, you've got to allow a lot of dissent. In fact, you have to foster dissent. One of my principles is that if I can't defend it, I shouldn't be doing it. What point is there in mindless agreement? I won't accept "Yes Sir!" for an answer. When you're working in these companies, you're with people who are older than you, younger than you, smarter than you. You have to remember that the board made you the boss, but your people make you the leader.

As you might imagine, debates have often become spirited inside the companies that Bill's managed. But that's par for the course at Electronic Elite companies. When managers yell, employees yell right back at them. Bill Campbell commented on this:

> I like people to fight back, and I hate people who just say "yes." I've got a temper, you know. I'm angry a lot—not abusive. But when I'm in your face, I expect you to come back at me with "Shit, Bill, I looked at it that way. It didn't work that way." That is ultimate management, in my view. I want people who aren't afraid to tell me what the hell's going on. You've got to be able to talk about it. I want you to hear me, and I want me to hear you. We're all interested in that one goal, the ultimate goal—making this company better.

The Electronic Elite create a work atmosphere in which issues can be discussed openly, without undue concern about treading on toes or violating turf. In an Electronic Elite organization, people generally aren't respected because of *position* but because of *contribution*. According to a 1994 article in *Wired* magazine, a hot programmer at Microsoft may have far more clout than an executive. This creates a true meritocracy, where a higher level of contribution creates a higher level of influence. Mitchell Kertzman, CEO of Powersoft, pointed out:

> You need a culture where (a) it's possible to put any crackpot idea on the table, (b) it's appropriate to say it's a crackpot idea, but (c) that can never translate into a negative comment on the individual who

put it on the table. So, people must have the courage to put things on the table and the courage to take the criticism when it comes. But, that's the kind of environment we have. It's a demanding, stimulating, tough environment. We had a management meeting recently when we discussed this very issue. There were some expressions of concern that maybe we were too tough on some people and some ideas. We talked it through and decided that this should remain a place where ideas get thrown into the cauldron and get mixed around. What always seems to come out of that process— painful though it may be—is great strategies, great products, and great ideas.

STRATEGY 9: BUILD AUTONOMOUS TEAMS

Dispersing power throughout an organization requires more than just encouraging dissent. It requires an organizational vehicle that can absorb and utilize power. Microsoft has a culture that does just that. Bill Gates remains a pervasive influence, but much decision making is done by employee teams, according to former Microsoft executive vice president Mike Maples:

> We organize into small teams. We have clear goals and objectives and missions for each team, and then we consciously don't have anyone watching them. There's nobody to report when they're not doing what they said they'd do—other than themselves. Part of the secret is behaving like you're small, allowing the teams to behave as if they're independent, as if they're small businesses themselves. They make many of their own decisions. Our development process doesn't require them to get signoff along the way.

At Microsoft, teams generally have near-total responsibility for their success or failure. They're expected to do whatever it takes to make their product successful, without meddling advice from corporate headquarters. Mike Maples continued:

> If Bill [Gates] or I or some of the other senior managers want to review where the teams are, we can ask to do so, but the teams never have to wait until they've been reviewed. If we don't get involved, they just go from start to finish by themselves. We've tried

to create an environment where people are responsible to themselves for their success. If you're clear on what their goals and objectives are at the beginning, and they understand what they're trying to accomplish and you understand what they're trying to accomplish, it works pretty well.

The Electronic Elite have found that small, autonomous teams are more likely to be responsive to customer needs. Small teams, too, are far less likely to develop the kind of inertia that keeps big organizations from adapting to changes in the market. Novell CEO Bob Frankenberg commented on this:

We have small teams that are going to be able to move product out the door without having to change everything else in the product. But the most important thing is to be able to get people who understand a set of needs better than anyone else in the world in a particular area, and then let them move to address that need. If you don't have the connection to the customer or the ability to handle the enormous amount of information that's involved, then you end up with a monolithic structure.

Organizing into small teams enables the Electronic Elite to function like small businesses. Each team has the necessary talent to make the product and the team successful. This frees the team to focus on what's important—the success of the product in terms of its ability to satisfy customer needs. Under these conditions, organizational politics become less important. Rather than kowtowing to review committees and turf protecting nabobs, the team can do whatever it takes to make its product a winner.

The idea that Management=Service allows Electronic Elite companies to give teams the autonomy that they need to get the job done. Electronic Elite leaders don't try to second-guess or review everything that their employees do. Hewlett-Packard CEO Lew Platt comments:

In organizations that have very tight controls, you usually find that the top management is prescribing how things will be done because there isn't the trust of individuals that makes it possible to give them freedom. [HP founders] Dave and Bill always emphasized that, as a manager, I work on *what* needs to be accomplished and leave it up to the individuals to figure out *how* to accomplish it. That's management by objectives, long before it was even called that. Again, it works well in an organization where you have enough confidence in the culture that it will put boundary conditions around the way people do things.

Points to Ponder

I recently attended a meeting of 20 chief information officers (CIOs) at which the subject of cross-functional teams was discussed in some detail. The CIOs who worked in traditional organizations were highly skeptical of the value of small teams. "We tried them, but they didn't work," was the most common comment. Traditional organizations often have enormous difficulty implementing decentralized organizations because their cultural mindsets don't provide the infrastructure for the strategy. The influence of culture on organizational strategy is shown in Figure 4.1.

Keeping Figure 4.1 in mind, consider the following questions about your organization and the impact that you can have on it:

• If you're a manager, how do you react under pressure? When you need to get things done, do you try to manipulate people to get what you want? Or do you encourage them to deal with the problem as they see fit?

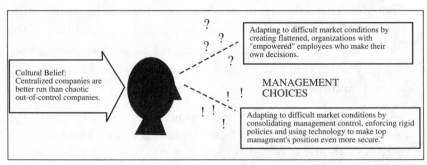

FIGURE 4.1. *Culture Limits Management Choices*

- How is your company organized? Does it have a complicated management hierarchy, or is power well distributed throughout the structure?
- If your organization is hierarchical, what were the market conditions that made such a structure a good idea? Have those conditions changed?
- Do people in the organization wait for the "bosses" to tell them what to do? If you're a manager, does this trouble you, or do you like the constant attention and feeling of being needed? If you're one of those who wait for the boss's orders, are you doing it out of habit, or out of fear?
- If your organization has cross-functional teams, does the team typically have to report to management, which then makes the decision? What would have to happen for your teams to be able to make decisions on their own?
- What would your company look like if it had less bureaucracy, or no bureaucracy at all? Would it be more productive? What would the managers and employees in your company have to believe about themselves to make bureaucracy a thing of the past?

Chapter Five

Employees as Peers

Earlier, we talked about how the employees of Electronic Elite companies work hard not only because they need to get their work done, but because they feel they're part of a community. We also talked about how Electronic Elite managers set up autonomous teams, a strategy that puts decision making where it belongs—closer to the customer. As noted, these concepts are put into practice under the umbrella of the Business=Ecosystem mindset, which encourages people to value cooperation over conflict and diversity over uniformity.

Also motivating the productivity and dedication of the Electronic Elite employee is the knowledge that he or she is regarded as a peer. A word heard frequently among Electronic Elite is *meritocracy*. Meritocracy is a system in which people are judged based on their achievements and contributions to an organization. A fancy title on a business card is not what determines someone's professional value.

The meritocracy as envisioned by the Electronic Elite also includes the notion that a person with merit is somebody who contributes to the best of his or her ability. This means that a truly excellent janitor is as deserving of respect as a truly excellent vice president. Frank Ingari, CEO of Shiva, explained:

In my opinion, if a job deserves to be done, then it deserves the equivalent respect of any other job. That's a core value. And I think that this applies not only in work, but in personal life. Let's say you've got a relative who is a truck driver. Well, why is he a truck driver? Is he good at it? Does he enjoy himself? Does he give time to his kids? Don't judge a person based on these arbitrary notions of how someone chooses his or her trajectory in life or what he or she happens to have been given genetically. I'm not trying to give you an egalitarian message. All I'm trying to say is make sure you don't value people according to arbitrary society values, because that's all ephemeral.

The concept of Employee=Peer promotes the notion that nobody is inherently superior to anybody else; therefore no one person should be ordering everyone else around. Hence, our truly excellent and respected janitor doesn't need to be constantly watched or supervised, because it's assumed that he or she is self-motivated enough to do the job well. That also means that you can afford to pay the janitor more because it reduces the need for a supervisor to look over the janitor's shoulder.

In addition to promoting respect between employees, the Employee=Peer mindset strengthens teamwork. When employees are assumed to be fundamentally equal, an employee may be a leader one day, and a follower the next. This makes it easier to form teams to accomplish short-term tasks, without posturing over who's top dog. When an employee is a peer, that employee will tend to strive for personal excellence and still take the time to help other employees achieve their goals. Employees with this level of confidence then are comfortable vying for the most difficult projects, setting ambitious deadlines, and basking in their teams' successes.

This is a very different approach from that currently in many companies, where managers try to control employee behavior. In traditional companies, it's common for managers to treat employees either as if they are children who have to be watched all the time. And what's particularly dangerous about the Employee=Child mindset is that it can become a self-fulfilling prophecy.

THE TRADITIONAL MINDSET: EMPLOYEE=CHILD

The labor practices that developed from Employee=Child mindset originated in Europe during the early years of the Industrial Revolution and were defined by a strict class system. Factory owners were aristocrats who were regarded by themselves and by society as superior to the laborers they hired. Just as landed gentry had instituted serfdom, factory owners saw laborers as tools with which to produce their goods. The more "kindly" factory owners treated laborers as children, who needed to be guided and disciplined. In fact, in many factories at that time, a majority of the laborers *were* children. By the time child labor was outlawed, the die was cast: employees were treated as if they still were immature, somehow "lesser" beings.

This attitude neatly dovetails with the Business=Battlefield mindset. Throughout history, armies have recruited primarily from the young, who are more impressionable and easily molded. It further connects to and reinforces the Management=Control belief.

Trust is at issue here, too. Traditionally, companies define complicated rules, procedures, and guidelines to govern nearly every aspect of working life. These rules suggest to employees that they are not trustworthy, lack common sense, and have even less capacity for making important decisions. This is what creates micromanagement. Employees who "break the rules" or "misbehave" are considered insubordinate and must be disciplined, like disobedient children.

Let us not forget that employees are people who drive cars, have sex, vote, have children of their own, and manage to lead their lives without the benefit of a corporate "parent." Paternalistic corporate behaviors go largely unexamined, however, because the Employee=Child mindset is so ingrained into the dominant corporate culture.

As mentioned, the infantilization of the workforce can become a self-fulfilling prophecy. Put simply, when you treat people like children, they act like children. Disgruntled from the absence of trust and disgusted with management's patronizing attitude, employees unintentionally become participants in a corporate culture where it's tempting to waste money, waste time, or even steal company property. Frank Ingari, CEO of Shiva, commented on this phenomenon:

> One of my first jobs outside of my father's company was with Western Electric. It was fascinating. We went to the office in the morning and got our assignments for the day from a computer. I was a cable monkey and, every day, they'd give us all the cables we were going to lay that day and how many minutes it would take us to do the job, all of which would add up to eight hours worth of work. When we finished that work, we were done for the day. Well, you can imagine, these cable guys weren't stupid. They never, ever, finished a job early. People were "disconnected" from the company. Nobody regarded the phone company as "our" company. That was the farthest thing from our minds. There was no distinction between the phone company, the post office, or IBM. The phone company was a bunch of WASP guys who pulled up in their Cadillacs and bland governmental stuff that we didn't understand. That feeling of disconnection results in the worst kind of sabotage. It's worse than theft. It's just not giving a shit. The only time you care is when you're being watched—if then.

The situation becomes cyclical. Soon, not only is management treating employees like children, but the employees are acting like children. Managers and employees become trapped in a dysfunctional relationship that makes high levels of productivity virtually impossible.

And it isn't just manual laborers who are treated this way. White collar employees, too, in many companies are suspected of stealing office supplies, so management locks the supply cabinets, forcing employees to fill out a form to get a pen or printer cartridge. The absence of trust is implicit. And locking up office supplies forces people to spend valuable work time just accessing the tools they need to do their jobs. This is seen as necessary, however, otherwise employees (children) will be dipping into the corporate cookie jar. I know of not one but two traditional computer vendors whose top management issued companywide memoranda complaining about the overuse of paper clips! Try to imagine, in the real world, a conversation between two adults where one suggests that the other should use fewer paper clips.

Another way managers insult employees is to reward themselves, even while expecting employees to implement cost-savings. For example, I worked for a company that had gotten itself into financial difficulties and consequently initiated a series of draconian cost controls. The president of the company delivered a speech via companywide closed-circuit television, which we listened to in a wired-up conference room. After making a few remarks about company loyalty and the importance of saving money, the president announced that he was accepting a substantial pay raise. A stunned silence filled the room. People started gathering up their notebooks and leaving the room before the broadcast was over. What was fascinating was that the president had no idea that he was giving a double message. Whatever incentive his employees might have had to save money was totally lost.

In direct contrast, the Electronic Elite employees are considered peers, contributors with full responsibility for their success and failure. This contrast is broken down clearly in Table 5.1.

TABLE 5.1. *Comparison of Child and Peer Mindsets*

EMPLOYEE=CHILD	EMPLOYEE=PEER
Identity. The ideal employee is a docile conformist, a real "team player" who will obey the rules.	*Identity.* The ideal employee is self-motivated and flexible, and does whatever it takes to make the team successful.
Organization. Structures are set up to control and supervise employee behavior to ensure that all the rules are followed.	*Organization.* People form small teams that have complete responsibility for their success within the context of the company's mission.
Motivation. Employees are assumed to want a reasonable salary, job security, and a company to take care of them.	*Motivation.* Employees want to change the world and make a difference, with the possibility of making big money somewhere down the line.

Electronic Elite managers focus on maintaining this peer structure by hiring people who will be good additions to the exiting staff. The Electronic Elite know that it takes constant effort to keep the Employee=Peer mindset active and alive within the corporate culture. Here are three of their strategies:

- Hire the self-motivated.
- Eliminate fancy perks.
- Encourage informality.

Let's look at each of these strategies in more detail.

STRATEGY 10: HIRE THE SELF-MOTIVATED

Being a peer means taking responsibility for your own actions. It takes a special kind of employee to feel comfortable and secure with this attitude. In particular, it requires the ability to stay self-motivated without a supervisor or manager looking over your shoulder. Former Microsoft executive vice president Mike Maples commented on Microsoft's employees:

> We find people who are very self-motivated, who set their own targets, and then drive themselves to achieve their goals. They're intellectually honest, if you will, in terms of training themselves to do better. We look for people who are leaders, who not only are self-motivated but who can help motivate other people.

Traditional companies also look for people who are self-starters, but generally only for positions such as sales that are conducted outside the corporate environment. The Electronic Elite look for self-motivated people at *all* levels of the organization, even for positions that traditional companies would consider low-level labor. Frank Ingari, CEO of Shiva, explained:

> Self-actualizing behavior is present in a significant minority of the population. It's people on the manufacturing line, the truck drivers, and everybody else. You have to treat them with respect.

Everybody's job has merit, and it's amazing what people will do just to be a part of a quality operation that delivers something tangible. People love that. They'll work beyond all expectation.

Frank makes an important point here that is echoed by many of his colleagues. *Everybody* is important, and an excellent company has to have excellence *everywhere*. That's possible only if everyone (including the people on the loading dock and the people who clean the floors) is doing a top-rate job, without being overseen by paternalistic bureaucrats.

Self-motivation also implies a high level of personal flexibility. This is vital because the duties of any job on an Electronic Elite team are likely to change on a week-to-week basis. Many positions don't even have written job descriptions. The idea is that everybody on the team does whatever it takes to get the job done, to get the product out, to make the customer happy. This requires people who are flexible enough to handle ambiguity and, sometimes, chaos.

One member of the Electronic Elite who understands this well is Jonathan Seybold. Jonathan is the founder and past president of Seybold Seminars, an organization that is responsible for some of the most innovative and well-attended trade shows in the computer industry. I often think of Jonathan as an industry guru because he's had such an enormous influence on the high-tech world and he continues to play an important role as a visionary and influencer of industry trends. Jonathan commented on the type of person who's a good fit for an Electronic Elite organization:

There are people for whom order and continuity and predictability are very important. They're like pets who resent absolutely any variation from their daily routine. At the other end of the spectrum are people who are basically anarchists. Along that continuum are people who like making sense of things but who are comfortable with ambiguity. Life itself can be ambiguous! I try to hire people who can deal with that.

Just as there are types of prospective employees that the Electronic Elite seek out, there are those they tend to avoid. For example, Electronic Elite companies generally don't hire the "professional managers" that are so common in the upper echelon of many of today's companies. An MBA doesn't count for much in the world of the Electronic Elite. What does count is a solid understanding of products, technology, and the customer needs. This requires a certain level of technical understanding that the so-called professional manager is likely to lack. Former Microsoft VP Mike Maples explained:

> We look for people who are highly skilled in their area, but more important, who are extraordinarily smart and can learn. If somebody says he or she is a programmer, we test him or her. But, often, we'll hire somebody who's not that good a programmer, say, but who's smart and willing to commit to learning. But, we don't hire very many people to come in as managers. People are hired as marketing people, or as programming people, or as content specialists, but not typically as professional managers.

The trend against hiring professional managers is based on a concern that such people function professionally in ways that make sense in traditional environments but that are not acceptable in an Electronic Elite organization. Such techniques tend to create dissent and anger, thereby disconnecting employees from the higher goals of the corporation. The traditional manager is likely to insist on the same kind of exaggerated respect and obedience that a subordinate historically has shown a "superior," rather than the mutual respect that exists between peers.

The Electronic Elite are looking for employees who are entrepreneurs. They want people who love what they do and are motivated by doing it. Frank Ingari, CEO of Shiva, defined what he considers the most valuable kind of employee:

> I had a guy in here yesterday. He's 29 years old. He's one of the head architects in the company. He's had no management training, none at all. I'm trying to find out what drives the guy, because he's a very important person for us to maintain and

motivate. He doesn't really care about the money, he just loves building products. Now that's obviously the gem you're looking for because he's a born entrepreneur.

Because the Electronic Elite want people who are "born entrepreneurs," they recruit people who can adapt to a new corporate culture without having to unlearn a lot of bad habits. This can often mean favoring youth and enthusiasm over age and experience. Hewlett-Packard CEO Lew Platt explained:

Historically, we've tried to recruit top students from top schools. While we do some experienced recruiting, the bulk of it is from college graduates. We find that people who have not spent a lot of time out in the work world come on board and buy into the culture. A lot of things around here just happen because that is the right way to do things at HP. Bringing in young people who don't have old cultural habits to shed before taking on our culture seems to work best for us. Beyond that, we look probably for the same things that other companies look for. That means people who are smart and have the focus to accomplish things. We look for people who are good communicators, who can work well in teams, because more and more, work in companies today is done by teams, not by individuals.

Electronic Elite companies generally have long and complex preemployment interviews. It's not unusual for a prospective candidate to interview not just with his or her manager but with prospective peers as well. If the candidate is being considered for a management job, typically, the candidate is interviewed by the people who will report to him or her. These extensive interviews make certain that the candidate will fit into the culture and into the team. As Jonathan Seybold put it:

When you hire people, you have to pay attention to how they're going to fit in. Someone can be a great person, but if he or she is not going to fit into the culture or the team, he or she is the wrong person. In this organization, there is a low tolerance for people who are political, who do not contribute to the team effort, or whose influence is negative. The focus is on getting the job done, and we simply don't have the time for people who violate that.

STRATEGY 11: ELIMINATE FANCY PERKS

When employees and managers are expected to team up and treat one another as peers, it's obviously hypocritical if the corporation treats some team members (the managers) better than it treats the other team members. This is precisely the reason many Electronic Elite organizations limit fancy management perks. Gone are executive washrooms and dining rooms, big offices, and limos that signaled to management and rank and file that managers are superior to workers and thus deserve special treatment. Perks also further isolate executives from the employees, exacerbating the hierarchy. Mitchell Kertzman, CEO of Powersoft, commented on the need for a consistent message here:

> It's not fair to expect employees to stay at a Motel 6 while the senior executives are flying around in corporate jets and golfing at the country club. I don't believe that everybody should wear sackcloth, but you've got to be consistent in your message and what you ask people to do. You don't want your average employee thinking that his or her wasting money on a daily basis is irrelevant in the scheme of things compared with executive compensation, executive travel, and executive perks.

Some CEOs, Novell's Bob Frankenberg for one, don't even have private offices. Bob has a cubicle like everybody else at Novell. Obviously, it isn't that Electronic Elite companies can't afford these extras, it's that a synonym for perks in this context is separateness. I asked Bob Frankenberg if he missed the luxuries that he might have enjoyed at a more traditional firm:

> Fancy perks actually make me feel very uncomfortable. I think that each of us has a job to do, and there isn't any job that isn't important. Or, if there is, then we shouldn't be doing that job. I consider just that we have different roles; this is not a hierarchy. We have an information system that allows me to implement this new structure. It's a great enabler for productivity.

Another good example of the employee as peer strategy is Minnesota-based EMD. With 900 employees and $160 million in yearly sales, EMD is one of the fastest-growing manufacturers of specialty computer boards, which are designed and built for individual customers. Sometimes EMD makes only a single board, designed for a very special purpose. This means that EMD must remain flexible at all times, so that the resources of the company can be marshaled at any moment to undertake a new and different project, big or small.

The president and CEO of EMD is Dr. David Fradin. A former professor of management science, David is a thoughtful man who's mastered the ability to lead an organization without controlling the behavior of the people within it. David told me that one of the secrets to EMD's productivity is the complete absence of the perks that would only serve to separate him from his employees.

> We're a company that has no offices. We have no reserved parking spaces. I'm CEO and president of EMD Associates, and I don't have a secretary who reports directly to me. We have an organization composed of approximately 150 teams. Some of them are very effective; others wander, looking for direction. But team organization and a team approach have become a standard part of the way we deal with a lot of issues. We don't believe in using the compensation system as a reward or punishment for performance. We're very egalitarian. I walk out on the production floor and people feel very comfortable walking up to me and making suggestions about virtually any business issue.

STRATEGY 12: ENCOURAGE INFORMALITY

Traditionally, formal relations between managers and workers emphasized the differences between the bosses and peons, enforcing the parent–child relationship that the Electronic Elite are determined to avoid. Informality, on the other hand, lets people relax around each other and treat one another as equals.

One way to create a sense of informality within a company is to encourage people to dress casually. For the past 15 years, Electronic Elite employees—management and staff alike—have rarely dressed in traditional business suits. Instead, business is comfortably carried on by people wearing T-shirts, sneakers, and blue jeans. This isn't to say that the Electronic Elite never wear suits. (In fact, when I interviewed Mitchell Kertzman, he was wearing an elegant business suit, albeit accessorized with red suspenders emblazoned with Mickey Mouse heads.) The point of not having a dress code isn't to replace one uniform with another. The idea is for people to dress however they feel is appropriate and however they feel comfortable. Wear a suit if you must, or dress down. It doesn't matter.

Dan Cerutti, a former IBM executive who started his own software company, explained:

> What I wear is important. I go into work dressed casually because I find this to be an extremely beneficial aspect of the new culture. It's more comfortable, it's more informal. IBM and many other companies tend to be stuffy. I learned a long time ago that not wearing an expensive suit tells the engineers and the first-level people that you're just a normal person. When you dress like a normal person instead of some big business magnate, your employees see you as much more approachable.

Casual dress echoes the casual way that people treat one another. Ceremony and ritual are replaced by comfortable interchanges that are much more productive than when communicating via a formal protocol. Michael Dell, CEO of Dell Computers, commented on the casual nature of the culture in his company:

> It's open and not particularly formal in terms of orientation. I'd say it's much more of a meritocracy than at other companies. People don't go around calling each other "Mr." and "Ms." Everybody calls one another by his or her first name. You can show up for work in blue jeans if you want to. There are areas of the company where no one ever wears a tie. There are certainly no assigned parking spaces or executive anythings. It's basically an open, free-form culture where you can bump into everybody and talk. I get e-mail all the time from people everywhere in the company. And I always send them a message back.

Being on a first-name basis may seem like a small thing, but it's symbolic of the relationships that the Electronic Elite try to create with the people in their organizations. By contrast, many traditional executives often insist on formality and would be very unsettled indeed, if a "subordinate" used his or her first name. I recently heard a rumor about an executive who left IBM to work for a company where first names were used throughout all levels of staff. When this executive held his first meeting, an employee addressed him as Ed. The executive reportedly interrupted: "Now that I'm working here, I expect you to show some respect. From now on, call me 'Mister'!" The employee thought it over for a second, shrugged, and said: "Whatever you say, Mister Ed."

The Electronic Elite believe that their effectiveness as managers is directly dependent on their ability to keep people connected to the goals of the organization. To do this, they relinquish divisive terminology and dress codes in favor of a general sense of informality that encourages employees to treat each other as self-motivated peers.

POINTS TO PONDER

The work experience need not demean the individual. By replacing the nineteenth century Employee=Child mindset with the twenty-first century Employee=Peer concept, the Electronic Elite have created a culture where individualism results in productivity, flexibility—and profit. Frank Ingari, President of Shiva, commented:

> The idea that you can spend most of your waking life and creative energies in an environment where you basically don't give a damn about the people you're working with and playing by rules you really don't agree with is loathsome! But it's what most people have had to live with for a long time in industrial society. For me, the idea of creating a new environment where people can tap into their creative energies and collaborative skills, and constantly learn, improve themselves, have fun, have broadening experiences, and travel is extraordinarily exciting!

With all this in mind, consider the following questions about your career and your place in your organization:

- Is your employee manual full of rules and regulations? Can you identify the core beliefs of the people who wrote the employee manual? How much of it was written 10, 15, or 20 years ago? Would your organization be less productive or more productive if it had a one-page employee manual?

- Are you self-motivated? How about the people you work with? How does it make you feel when management intervenes and tells you to do things that you already know that you have to do? Do you become more motivated or less motivated? What does this say about the nature of control and power in an organization?

- Do most of the employees in your organization enjoy their jobs? Do they add to their lives or does working just take a big bite out of their time? How could you help motivate the people you work with so that they'll feel more dedicated to the organization's goals?

- How much more productive do you think your company would be if people really believed that they were peers who shared in the success of the entire team? What's stopping you from implementing this?

- How formal is your organization? Do people wear uniforms? Are workers on a first-name basis with management? If not, why do you think that the managers want or expect to be treated differently? Is the formality something that helps productivity, or is it just a sign of insecurity on the part of management?

- Are perks part of the management compensatory package in your organization? Does everyone enjoy them, or just a privileged few? Are the perks supposed to be an incentive for people? What message does this give to the average worker?

Chapter Six

Motivate with Vision

Unquestionably, the most successful Electronic Elite leader in the computer industry is Bill Gates, cofounder and chairman of Microsoft, the world's largest independent software company. Bill is both a visionary and a master at getting other people to share his vision of the future. Today, Bill has all the resources of a giant corporation at his back and can spend millions of dollars promoting his vision. But all that power is simply an extension of what Bill has been doing since he was a young boy. Bill's early years as a programmer helped him mold his vision:

> My interest in computers began early, and I started programming in high school at age 13. When I was at Harvard in 1974, Paul Allen and I began the development of BASIC for the first microcomputer, the MITS Altair. Even then we were convinced that the personal computer would ultimately become a valuable tool found on every office desktop and in every home. We saw that a microcomputer revolution was underway, and we left Harvard the following year to form Microsoft in pursuit of that vision.

As Microsoft grew, Bill's vision grew along with it. He has likened the process of building a great company to that of building a program. First comes the vision, which provides the motivation, and then comes the discipline to make the vision into a reality.

The ability to recognize opportunities is essential to success in this fast-moving industry. A healthy dose of vision has been central to development of Microsoft. Every decision we make is based on where we think the technology will be 5 and 10 years in the future. Our programming experiences prepared us well for a managerial role. The programmer's ability to envision a strong product and methodically map out the code that must be written to build it is analogous to the manager's ability to envision a strategic new line of business and delineate the appropriate steps to create it.

According to Bill, one of the reasons that the traditional computer vendors were unable to adapt was that they lost their sense of vision and therefore failed to change as the market did:

In this leadership role, I am constantly reminded of the need for clear vision and strong execution. Many companies that were once great powers in this business have lost their way. Fixated on the technology that made them great, they were not able to extend their reach into new areas. At Microsoft I make sure we don't fall short for not having an expansive view of how technology can be used.

Another member of the Electronic Elite who believes in the power of vision is Eckhard Pfeiffer, the CEO of COMPAQ. When Eckhard took over the leadership of COMPAQ, the company was in decline. Once famous for developing the best personal computers in the industry, it had lost its edge and was losing market share. Eckhard, however, had a vision of what COMPAQ could be. He not only believed that COMPAQ could pull itself out of the doldrums, he knew that COMPAQ had potential for new growth. He wasn't satisfied with keeping COMPAQ in the number three market share position in PC sales after industry giants IBM and Apple. Instead, he believed that COMPAQ could be number one in market share. Within two years, he had turned that vision into a reality. Eckhard commented:

From a CEO's perspective, you're taking on a very large responsibility. Ultimately, it's people that make everything happen. That's what we keep saying, but at times we forget it. You have a responsibility to shape the vision of a company, and you know that whatever process you choose will determine ultimately the well-being of the organization. You have to drive that vision and long-term strategies and objectives. You deal with it on a day-to-day basis. And you always have to remember that your competitors are doing the same thing. They're working as intensely on all these things as well. The element of success is a satisfaction and gratification for putting in the effort.

A sense of vision, according to members of the Electronic Elite, shared among the employees in an organization, is the best way to motivate people. Of course, they aren't the only business leaders who understand the power of vision. The ability to share a vision is a quality that all great leaders share, including traditional ones. What the Electronic Elite do differently is that they avoid the use of fear to motivate employees.

THE TRADITIONAL MINDSET: MOTIVATE = FEAR

Probably the most dysfunctional concept of traditional corporate culture is that it's appropriate, even beneficial, to control workers with fear. This concept arises naturally out of the other mindsets that we've discussed already. If the function of management is to control worker behavior, and the way to view employees is as children, then management needs a tool with which to keep the children in line. And, historically, that tool has been fear.

In the past, and today as well, many managers hold the threat of firing or demotion over employees' heads. The message is clear: "Work hard or you're outta here!" The tone was set in the nineteenth century. Anyone who refused (or was unable) to work 14-hour days, seven days a week, was unceremoniously dismissed, only to be replaced by another—to the manager—faceless, nameless laborer.

The all too obvious strong-arm tactics were abandoned by the mid-twentieth century. IBM, for example, became known for its policy of lifetime employment. Once you were hired by IBM, you had a steady job for the rest of your life, as long as you followed the rules. IBM, like other companies that promised such security, has been unable to deliver on that promise. Recent changes in the economy have made the concept of a steady job nothing more than a memory. Millions of workers have lost their jobs as a result of downsizing, rightsizing, outsourcing, and reengineering. This resurgence of insecurity in the workplace has reawakened the fear of joblessness in many workers in all fields.

Fear makes companies less competitive and adaptable, and causes workers to become less, rather than more, productive. When people are afraid, they will avoid taking necessary risks. I've worked with companies whose employees are so afraid that it's a miracle anything gets done at all. People in these organizations become paralyzed and won't take any action whatsoever lest they be blamed if it goes awry. Managers start demanding detailed plans for everything in a vain attempt to guarantee that nothing goes wrong. What usually happens in these cases is that the organization ends up studying the possible outcomes of an opportunity so long that the opportunity ceases to exist. Computer industry guru Jonathan Seybold commented:

> In traditional organizations, people were often punished for taking risks that didn't pan out. Consequently, the major activity in the organization was deflecting blame. So you send memos, you hold meetings, all to make certain that you are "clean." I've seen this to be the case even when the organization was full of bright, literate, intelligent human beings. The culture starts to run them, not the other way around.

The climate of fear in many companies slows decision making to a crawl while everyone seeks to cover his or her behind. Distrust leads to bureaucracies that insist on checking every last detail. Tasks that, in a reasonable organization, could be handled in a few hours, in such an organization might take days, weeks, or months, or never be completed.

At the minicomputer and mainframe vendors in the 1980s, for example, a product couldn't even be considered for prototyping until there was an engineering plan, a marketing plan, a sales plan, a competitive analysis, a release plan, a master plan, and a project plan, all of which had to be reviewed and approved by multiple departments and bureaucracies. Since it literally took months to create and review all these documents, it was rarely possible to get products launched in a timely fashion, which is critical in that market. In addition, the homework had to be repeated at each stage of the development process, so that a product was never complete until it had hundreds of signatures and sign-offs. Projects that should have taken months stretched into years, or got caught in an endless maze of paperwork and politics. And, by the time the rare product actually did get built, it was out of date.

Fear also degrades the quality of communications inside an organization. In an effort to deflect potential blame, employees engage in double-talk and "weasel words." Whenever you see a memorandum that's a soup of industry buzzwords and half-truths, carefully crafted to spread blame and communicate next to nothing, you can bet that there's a terrified executive or two cowering nearby. Here's an example:

> After due consideration of alternatives, we take calculated risks based on a wise assessment of market conditions.

No doubt, the executives who wrote this felt that they were making a strong statement. But between the lines, the message is: "We don't take risks."

One of the most ridiculous manifestations of motivation by fear is a function called "group writing." A group of professionals sit together in a meeting and try to write a paragraph. In the quest for perfect phrasing, they debate and comment on each word. It can take an hour to do a single sentence, a day to do a paragraph. The reason for this bizarre ritual is to make certain that everyone is "happy" with the wording, meaning that everyone agrees to share the blame for what it says. And if *everyone* shares the blame, then *no one* is responsible if things go wrong.

The result of double-talk and group writing is that people in an organization stop valuing truth, even if they can still recognize it. Information that is difficult for the culture to absorb gets buried

DILBERT reprinted by permission of United Feature Syndicate, Inc.

and avoided. Over time, managers and employees alike lose track of what's going on in the market because everybody's afraid to state the facts.

Employees who are afraid don't make good decisions, they don't take well-considered risks, and they don't act rationally. Go into almost any conference room in a traditionally run company and you'll see them. They glance around the room frequently, waiting and worrying, laughing a little too loudly when the boss cracks a feeble joke, agreeing with whatever idea seems popular or politically correct.

In contrast, Electronic Elite proponents believe that their companies succeed or fail on the ability—and willingness—of their employees to take intelligent risks. They know there simply isn't time in this fast-changing economy to study a problem to death, to engage in complicated consensus building, or to be afraid. Bold behavior is impossible when people in an organization are fearful of the consequences if they make a mistake. Consequently, the Electronic Elite don't expect perfection from their employees. They only expect people to learn from their mistakes. Powersoft CEO Mitchell Kertzman comments:

> I can't imagine motivating people through fear. You don't want people afraid of the consequences if they screw up. I want them to do the right thing, but if they try to do the right thing and fail, I still want them to try. Everybody is allowed mistakes. That's not to say that people are allowed to make the same mistake over and over again. The first mistake is almost always forgiven, especially if the person can learn from the experience.

> You don't want people to work in a risk-averse culture. You don't want someone, for example, to come up with an idea and have everybody else in the room say (or imply): "That's the dumbest thing I've ever heard and, boy, are you a stupid person." If you do that, the person will never again come up with an idea for fear that it might be laughed at. We have a very demanding culture, and ideas get put on the table, including my own, to which people say, essentially, "that's a dumb idea," but they're not saying "you're a stupid person."

Rather than increasing the level of fear in the organization, the Electronic Elite seek to minimize it. They want employees to feel that they are in charge of their destiny—not waiting for the proverbial axe to drop. They want employees to claim ownership for their decisions, not seek to pass or share blame. This means that they must depend on a shared vision, rather than on fear, to

TABLE 6.1. *Comparison of Fear and Vision Mindsets*

MOTIVATION = FEAR	MOTIVATION = VISION
Mistrust and Distrust. Fear makes it difficult to trust your colleagues, peers, and employees, who are assumed either to be enemies or (at best) temporary allies.	*Trust.* A shared vision makes it easier to trust the colleagues who share your hopes and dreams in the context of the organization's larger goals.
Predictability. Frightened people don't like surprises, so they set up structures to make sure that everything remains completely under control, that is, unchanging.	*Courage.* A shared vision encourages people to take necessary risks and to do what it takes to make the vision into a reality.
Deceptiveness. In fearful organizations, employees consider it appropriate and even wise to deflect blame by fabricating or omitting information.	*Decisiveness.* A shared vision creates a work environment in which decisions can be made quickly and easily because it's clear how each decision fits into the overall vision.

provide the primary motivation. The different effects of Motivation=Fear and Motivation=Vision are shown in Table 6.1.

The impact of Motivation=Fear shows itself most clearly in the quality of life in the corporation. Fear always makes employees miserable and unhappy.

My personal experience tells me that work in an Electronic Elite organization can be a wonderful and positive experience. My first job was at the Los Angeles Development Center, an organization that was ahead of its time in terms of its organizational culture. Dress was casual, everyone was on a first-name basis, and crack programmers held more power than managers. Most important, the group had a mission that permeated every aspect of daily working life. This mission consisted of a commitment to achieve a goal that no software development organization had ever done before—rewrite the programming code for a complex, multiuser operating system so that it would run on a completely different hardware platform. It was a project that many computer scientists considered impractical, if not impossible, especially in the time frame (three years) allotted.

Rather than being daunted by the size of the task, we were empowered by a sense of adventure, for we were exploring new ground, accomplishing something unique. Motivated by that vision, we worked long hours, often 50 to 60 a week, and yet few of us were conscious of how hard we were working. And on Monday mornings, we looked forward to going back to work. My job was far from the most important in the organization (I was a new hire just out of college), but I was made to feel as if I were an essential part of the teams on which I served. I was free to attend any meeting that interested me or at which I felt I could make a contribution. The camaraderie spilled over into our personal lives; there was a party nearly every weekend, where we'd socialize and talk about the next stage of the development process.

The entire focus of the organization was getting a product out the door. There were about 100 programmers, and only four secretaries. The managers were all former programmers who were capable of making technical contributions. Even the technical writers were expected to know how to program.

The ultimate payback came when we accomplished what had seemed to outsiders to be impossible. Not only did we convert the operating system to the new hardware platform, but we did it on schedule, hitting a deadline that had been set three years earlier. It was an extraordinary triumph and garnered major financial benefits for the parent company.

Whenever I talk to people in Electronic Elite companies, I sense this same level of energy, dedication, and enthusiasm that is generated when people know that they're part of something special, that they're changing the world, if only in a small way. I can see how a Bill Gates (Microsoft), a Bob Frankenberg (Novell), or an Edward McCracken (Silicon Graphics) can inspire employees to ever-greater achievements.

The Electronic Elite have three strategies that help them motivate their employees with vision:

- Create a climate of trust.
- Create a sense of mission.
- Compensate for missions accomplished.

STRATEGY 13: CREATE A CLIMATE OF TRUST

When employees know that they're involved in growing something—rather than in an endless war over market share—their perspective has balance. When co-workers believe that they're part of a community, they view their colleagues as friends rather than competitors. And managers who don't try to control employee behavior reap the benefits of production inspired out of loyalty, not fear.

These are the components in a climate of trust, without which there can be no vision. Trust is the fertile ground in which the vision is planted. Software entrepreneur and former IBM executive Dan Cerutti commented:

> I've known bosses who distrust people and think they won't deliver. It comes through in everything they do. They're afraid to let go. They don't make people feel good. That was true at IBM, and it's still true at many companies. I prefer flat organizations, because you don't need a lot of managers if you trust in the people to do their jobs. It creates faster decision making. You get more autonomy and more responsibility closer to the people who actually know the details. It's these people who need to be empowered to make decisions, then they'll make decisions more quickly, and you get a faster heartbeat. You get people who are more responsible. You get everything I want.

Trust means letting employees make decisions even if those decisions aren't part of the company's normal practice. It also means that managers should let go of their fears of anything out of the ordinary. Powersoft CEO Mitchell Kertzman commented:

> Suppose I have an employee who's with a customer. It's late in the evening and the customer has a problem, and the employee—to do

the right thing for the customer—has to give him or her something or make a commitment that costs money. I want that employee to do the right thing for the customer, even if it's not
normal practice. He or she wouldn't get punished for that, even
though we might not normally make that kind of commitment. If
it was the right thing to do for that customer at that time, then it
was the right thing to do.

STRATEGY 14: CREATE A SENSE OF MISSION

A sense of mission is essential to the success of any organization.
Employees at successful companies have a clear understanding of
what they are trying to accomplish and use that understanding as a
touchstone for their everyday behavior. One way that the Electronic Elite create a sense of mission is by organizing employees
into teams that function like small businesses. This allows each
employee to see clearly that his or her action really makes a personal and professional difference.

The Electronic Elite also foster in their employees the belief
that if they can't change the world, they can at least make a difference. Sally Narodick, CEO of Edmark, commented on this:

> We look for self-actualized people who are very confident, have a
> tremendous amount to contribute, and who love the area in which
> we're working. Most of the people who come here love kids, are
> new to parenthood, or have kindergarten-age kids, and they're
> awed by the wonder and the potential of children. They identify
> with our value system and they want to join us to make a differ-
> ence and a contribution to the world.

Former Microsoft executive vice president Mike Maples added:

> Great companies have people who are smart, energetic, focused,
> dedicated to the company, and care about what they're doing;
> they believe that they really are on a mission to change things,
> and that they're doing what's right for the world and right for
> humankind.

Many organizations solidify their missions by developing mission statements. The following are examples of the terminology and thoughts used to inspire Electronic Elite employees:

- *Dell Computer.* Develop quality products and do whatever it takes to please the customer.
- *Shiva.* Provide secure, easy-to-use, scalable, and cost-effective remote access solutions that meet the needs of nontechnical end users and network managers alike.
- *Hewlett-Packard.* Provide products and services of the highest quality and the greatest possible value to our customers, thereby gaining and holding their respect and loyalty.
- *Knowledge Adventure.* Make really inspiring, compelling, exciting, multimedia, educational software for kids.

Note that all these informal mission statements highlight giving something important to the customer, providing a high level of quality, or performing an important service. Placing the mission statement in the context of changing the world—however small this change might be—engenders loyalty to the goals and purpose of the organization.

For the Electronic Elite, a mission statement is a crystallization of what the organization is trying to accomplish and why. The goal is to get people thinking about possibilities, rather than limitations. A strong mission statement inspires as much as it informs. Employees must feel that the organization has a goal beyond that of making a profit. A successful statement explains why the organization's products or services make sense not only from a financial viewpoint but also from the viewpoint of the organization's customers.

A good mission statement also brings people together. It describes how being connected with the larger organization has a positive social and career benefit. A good mission statement attracts people who will fit in the organization. When people join an organization, they should feel that they've become part of something that's special, that they have a unique and important purpose that is not only going to enrich their own lives, but make the world a better place.

STRATEGY 15: COMPENSATE FOR MISSIONS ACCOMPLISHED

As important as a vision is in achieving success, it won't pay the rent. Employees have to be compensated when the company succeeds. There's a tradition in Electronic Elite companies—especially start-ups—to give employees attractive stock options that, should the company or the project prove successful, can be far more valuable than a high salary. This allows smaller companies to attract top talent, even when they can't afford to pay them a lot of money up front.

Case in point is Knowledge Adventure, which develops multimedia educational software for children. Knowledge Adventure acquired its reputation by releasing some great products long before most computers were working with multimedia. The company took a big risk, but one that paid off, allowing Knowledge Adventure to become a serious and early contender in one of the most high-tech segments of the computer software business.

At Knowledge Adventure, employees are given a choice of how they want to be compensated, by a relatively higher salary and no "upside" stock potential, or by a lower salary, with a serious upside potential should the company do well. CEO Bill Gross explains:

> We generally pay salaries that are a little lower than marketplace. That's so we can grow at this rate and still maintain profitability. We have an unusual scheme for making offers to people. It seems logical, but I hadn't heard of it before. After we talk to people who have the passion about what we're doing here and who have the skills, we ask them about their needs and current economic position. Then we usually make them three offers: one is what they need to get by, plus some stock; the second is more than they need and less stock; the third is less than they need and more stock. By spelling these options out, everyone gets a sense of pitching in, whether it's in equity or dollars.

Compensation in Electronic Elite companies tends to be tied directly to the success of the company (if the company is small) or the success of a product (if the company is large). Electronic Elite leaders feel that this is essential to keep people connected to the organization. That connectedness is enhanced when the employee is convinced that his or her contribution directly impacts profitability. It obviously increases productivity when the employee knows that this contribution will result in a higher level of personal compensation.

Compensating based on missions accomplished also encourages an atmosphere of thrift, because compensation is tied to the profitability of the team's project. This creates a natural resistance to wasting money. Many Electronic Elite companies are among the most profitable in the world. Microsoft, for example, regularly achieves net margins in excess of 25 percent, a figure that's higher than the gross margins for many other industries.

Electronic Elite leaders build cost control into their cultures, so that each individual instinctively keeps an eye on the bottom line. Jonathan Seybold describes the way that he set up his Seybold Seminars company:

> We have a tradition of profit sharing. That was a goal from the start. I believe that the people who are making a business successful should share in that success. One of the consequences is that we've built a culture that is "cheap"—people don't waste money. I didn't realize it when I started, but one of the reasons that so many companies have problems controlling costs is that they try to control them from the top down—with rules and regulations. When you control costs from the bottom up, you don't need all of that. I didn't start profit sharing for that reason, but it was one of the consequences. It breeds a very different kind of organization.

POINTS TO PONDER

The Electronic Elite have created organizations that inspire employees with a vision that's built on enthusiasm and joy. Sally Narodick, CEO of Edmark, said:

You've got to be in touch with what matters and let go of the other stuff and adjust your lifestyle to be able to afford the salary cut and get your joy where it's really meaningful, and recognize that taking those cuts is an investment that'll give you tremendous forward growth and joy.

Consider the following questions:

- Do you have a clear picture of what your organization is all about? Does it make you proud? If not, what would have to change for you to be proud of your organization?
- In your organization, are rewards and salaries tied to longevity and attendance, or to achievement and performance? How much more productive do you think your organization could be if people knew that they'd be rewarded much more lavishly if the organization truly fulfilled its mission?
- Are people in your organization often afraid? What is the source of that fear? What could you do today to make that fear less pervasive?
- Does your organization have a mission statement? Who wrote it? Do people understand it and use it as a touchstone for everyday behavior? If not, could it be that the vision and the mission aren't really clear enough?
- Do the people in your team make more money when the team is successful? Is there enough incentive for people to make the team work? Does everyone get the same benefits, or are certain "stars" singled out for extra reward? How does that affect the team?
- If you or somebody on your team saves the company money, is it reflected in your paycheck? Are people rewarded for saving money or penalized for not spending their entire budget at year's end? What would have to change for your organization to make "bottom-up" cost control a reality?

Chapter Seven

Change Is Growth

The Electronic Elite are the pioneers of the technological frontier, whose boundaries cannot be mapped, because they are constantly expanding. Bill Gates put it succinctly:

> The human experience is about to change. The transition will be exciting and historic, empowering to individuals, and brutal to some companies and institutions that don't keep pace. Even with the current information highway mania, the impact that emerging digital tools will have and the richness they will bring to people is wildly underestimated. Once certain thresholds are crossed, the way we work and live will change, forever.

Edward McCracken, CEO of Silicon Graphics, added:

> The computer industry is in its infancy even though it's been around for 40 or 50 years, depending on how you count it. I believe that advanced applications are just starting to be developed and that the next 10 or 20 years will be a wonderful time to try new things. And how wonderful and stimulating to be forced continually to change.

McCracken, Gates, and the rest of the Electronic Elite regard change as exciting, challenging, part of the "juice" of being in business. This attitude is an essential element in their success. They make change a part of their day-to-day business.

This posture enables Electronic Elite organizations to continually evolve to meet new circumstances. They transform themselves with relative ease, even when the change presents serious management challenges, such as necessary layoffs. Because the Electronic Elite have the mental framework that supports a positive view of change, they can make it serve their higher goals. Frank Ingari, CEO of Shiva, explained how this attitude differs from traditional approaches to change:

> One can deplore the current state of change. That's what the unions do; they have a wrong mental model of reality, of economic reality. Society at large has to embrace change, as opposed to embracing static thinking. Remember the conflict between the steelworkers and the steel mills? How quaint that battle seems today. People are finally realizing that major corporations are not omnipotent; the mighty have fallen. They've had to do horrendous layoffs and the management ended up looking like Bozos. The image of the omnipotent company in a static world making widgets is dead. Today, the reality is constant change and the challenge is who's going to reap the harvest of change.

The companies of the Electronic Elite are well positioned to harvest the fruits of change because they promote the belief that Change=Growth. That's very different from the dominant attitude of the past.

The Traditional Mindset: Change=Pain

Traditional corporate culture is skeptical and fearful of change. This attitude developed in the nineteenth century, which was a time of social and political turmoil, in the midst of which large corporations seemed like havens of stability. To this day, many corporations use the number of decades they've been in business to promote their value. They enshrine portraits of their founders on the walls of their boardrooms. It even slips into the vocabulary; it's not unusual to hear executives call their company "The Firm" as if to emphasize its rigidity.

To traditionalists, fundamental corporate change should be considered only when the "corporate machine" breaks down, or when the "army" loses the final "battle," or when the company becomes completely "out of control." Change is never regarded as positive; it's always a last resort.

On the other hand, even the most conservative traditionalists are now aware their corporations must change in order to adapt to new markets. This awareness, growing in the late 1980s and early 1990s, led to the popularity of two management techniques—reengineering and total quality management—each promising to help executives transform and update their organizations. However, the traditional corporation's emotional attachment to stability can easily frustrate even well-meaning change attempts.

As defined by Hammer and Champy, writing in *Reengineering the Corporation*, reengineering a company "means tossing aside old systems and starting over. It involves going back to the beginning and inventing a better way of doing work." While this sounds good, in practice reengineering has often proven difficult to implement. Even reengineering experts admit that reengineering isn't a panacea:

> We believe that the failure rate for reengineering is, in fact, much higher—on the order of 70 percent. Why do the best-laid reengineering plans often go astray? The causes are many. Despite bold initial pronouncements of shaking up the status quo, some companies end up merely tinkering with well-entrenched business processes. Others try to drive radical process change from the bottom up and quickly get stymied by functional managers defending parochial interests. And in a few organizations we have encountered, reengineering is just one more change program on the corporate agenda, eventually suffocating from lack of resources and attention. (Steven Stanton, Michael Hammer, and Bradford Power, quoted in *Insights Quarterly*, Fall Issue, 1992)

The reason that true reengineering is so difficult is that traditional corporate culture places such a high value on stability that radical change is simply too threatening to be taken on. The status quo must be defended at all costs, even if the status quo is slowly destroying profitability.

As a result, many reengineering efforts are doomed to be ineffective from the start. I once observed from a distance a reengineering effort conducted by a prestigious management consulting company. The organization being reengineered saw the consultants as intruders and there was massive resistance to the process. It quickly degenerated into a seemingly endless series of meetings, ostensibly to determine how the organization was currently performing. The output of these meetings was a gigantic stack of diagrams.

Further meetings took place in which the diagrams were redrawn to look as different as possible, even though the processes they described remained the same. A workflow originally shown as a straight line, for example, was redrawn as a "closed-feedback" circle, a tree-shaped organization chart was redrawn as an interconnected pyramid, and so forth. Important-sounding but ultimately meaningless buzzwords were liberally sprinkled throughout.

The entire reengineering effort had consumed thousands of valuable hours of employee time and had cost over a million dollars in consultant fees. However, the end result—a complicated and nearly unreadable report—was never acted on. The status quo remained impervious.

Total quality management (TQM) is another corporate change method that hasn't lived up to its promise. TQM was pioneered by the late W. Edwards Deming and Joseph Juran and was widely credited with improving Japanese manufacturing. It uses teams drawn from all parts of the company to define and solve problems, providing statistical analysis tools to track the progress of the change process.

However, despite its initial promise, TQM is beginning to look like a fad whose time has come and gone. In October 1995, *USA Today* ran a story headlined "Is TQM Dead?" It points out that applications for Baldridge awards—the "Oscar" of the TQM world—are down to 47 from a peak of 106 in 1991. The article cites "reengineering and disillusionment" as factors in this decline in popularity. A representative of the Deming Center for Quality Management at Columbia University, Peter Kolesar, put it this way: "A majority of companies that have gotten deeply involved in Total Quality have not made it pay off. When they don't see results quickly, they move on to something else." Frank Ingari, CEO of Shiva, commented:

> Top management does it as a fad. You know how it goes, the same company that did quality circles is now doing reengineering. Did they ever connect those two concepts? Did they ever consider that maybe the reengineering ought to be done by the people who are responsible for the work? How much of this effort increases people's feeling of connectedness to the company?

According to a 1994 poll cited in *Fortune* magazine, executives believe that less than one third of TQM efforts are anything more than a "flop." The most frequently mentioned barriers to change were "employee resistance and 'dysfunctional corporate culture.'" In other words, TQM (like reengineering) fails when the corporate culture leads employees to fear change.

Reprinted with special permission of King Features Syndicate.

When reengineering and TQM fail, then most companies are forced into the last resort—layoffs. It's widely believed that laying off workers will automatically improve profits by cutting costs. This is not always true, however. As early as October 1993, *The Wall Street Journal* was pointing out that "many companies that slash furiously still perform poorly—and can't figure out why." One reason for this failure of downsizing was that more than half of the companies surveyed ended up refilling positions within a year of eliminating them.

However, even when "downsized" positions aren't refilled, many companies don't receive the positive results that they expected.

According to downsizing expert Kenneth P. De Meuse of the University of Wisconsin, quoted in the same article, profits can decline faster after layoffs than before: "Not only is a reduction in force not a quick fix, as many companies believe, but it's most likely not a fix at all."

According to my observation, layoffs generally fail when they leave in place the structures and relationships that got the company into trouble in the first place. Such layoffs diminish whatever effectiveness the company might still have by reducing the number of people available to make the existing system work. The company tries to do more work with fewer employees, creating overwork, demoralization, and pointless political activity. Former IBM vice president Willy Shih had this to say on the subject:

> In big organizations, there tends to be a leadership vacuum. Most people aren't willing to put a stake in the ground and take some risks or take some aggressive actions to change things. As the organization shrinks and there are a lot of reorganizations, people start thinking: "Oh my God, what's my next job? Am I going to get laid off?" You find inordinate amounts of time being spent on reorganization. Why? Because people know how to do those. People don't know how to approach the much more difficult problem of getting sales and revenue up or getting costs down.

Nowhere was this problem more obvious than in the way that Honeywell Information Systems, one of the traditional mainframe vendors, downsized in the 1980s.

Case Study: Downsizing at Honeywell Information Systems

In 1982, the third largest computer company in the United States was Honeywell Information Systems (HIS), which included a profitable mainframe business that it had purchased from companies such as General Electric and Xerox. Although less than a sixth of the size of industry giant IBM, HIS was, in many ways, the most innovative of the traditional mainframe vendors. Its computers were extraordinarily secure and reliable, and its engineers developed a minicomputer long before the rest of the mainframe companies entered that market. HIS also had a tradition of excellence in software development.

In contrast to these powerful advantages, HIS also had some substantial weaknesses. Top management at HIS evidently knew little or nothing about computers; they were professional managers. Consequently, HIS had a Byzantine bureaucracy, lengthy chains of command, and the essential conservatism that comes along with the notion that change in inherently painful. Nevertheless, HIS was doing well in the early 1980s, selling computers in numbers that made the professional managers in the boardroom very happy indeed.

By 1988, however, HIS was on its last legs, the victim of the same market forces that we've been discussing throughout this book. Low-cost personal computers were replacing high-cost minicomputers and mainframes. The radical drop in the cost of computing power made it impossible to sell the big machines at the same inflated prices as before. Consequently, demand for HIS's mainframe products was declining rapidly.

Why didn't HIS leverage its financial power and installed base to tap the increasingly lucrative market for personal computers? The answer is that HIS, like most traditional companies, had a deep-seated fear of change. The market for personal computers was completely different from the market for mainframes. The machines were manufactured differently, shipped differently, sold differently, and supported differently. To be successful in this market, HIS would have had to remake itself, something that the managers at the top were unable to accomplish. HIS did make a deal with an off-brand manufacturer of personal computers to distribute its products, but HIS simply wasn't set up to take advantage of the new trends.

For HIS to have succeeded in the personal computer business, it would have had to change its manufacturing processes so that it could make its own PCs cost-effectively. Further, it would have had to establish relationships with dealers and distributors that sold PCs, and change its policies around pricing and support. In a company structure like Honeywell's, radical changes such as these would have taken years. They would have had to evolve slowly, with checks and balances, reviews and approvals.

Regardless of its fear, HIS's management finally had change thrust on them in its least palatable form. Its financial position weakened to the degree that it could remain profitable only if it reduced headcount. Thus, the HIS strategy was to protect the status quo for as long as possible.

The first series of layoffs, begun in 1986, took the form of voluntary retirements. The idea was to get the most senior—and the highest paid—workers to leave the company voluntarily. The retirement packages included a generous severance known as the "golden handshake." As a result of this offer, many of the brightest and most experienced people in the company left.

The second series of layoffs expanded the voluntary retirements to younger employees. As with the previous round of layoffs, Honeywell offered a generous severance package to those who were willing to leave, regardless of their role and contribution to the company. As you might expect, the people to accept this offer were those with the most up-to-date skills and the best connections in the industry. One former Honeywell employee put it this way:

> The more things changed, the more they stayed the same. The people who stayed were the ones who didn't have the skills to get a better job somewhere else. It was like an IQ test: if you were smart enough to get another job, Honeywell would pay you to take it.

Why would HIS strip the company of experience and talent just when it needed them most? These half-measures created the appearance of change—of movement toward profitability—without actually requiring anything to change.

Voluntary layoffs weren't sufficient, however. Profits kept dropping as demand for HIS's machines plummeted. Top management could see no other recourse than to launch a series of "across-the-board" layoffs. These layoffs weren't voluntary, but they were calculated to make as little impact as possible on Honeywell's underlying structure and mechanisms of control. The "across-the-board" lay-offs left the current system in place, but with fewer people. And unsurprisingly, each successive layoff further diminished HIS's effectiveness because it was trying to do the same amount of work and the same kind of work, but with fewer and fewer people.

This constant dribbling away of the company's lifeblood left the remaining employees in a state of constant fear, always waiting for the other shoe to drop. Innovation ground to a complete halt. As the layoffs continued, it became clear that only the politically savvy were surviving the carnage, and instead of focusing on turning the company around, employees spent their time and effort jockeying for a "safe" position. By 1990, Honeywell was staffed by confused employees wandering the halls like ghosts, waiting in misery for the pink slip. This debacle is diagrammed in Figure 7.1.

Eventually, Honeywell sold its computer business to Groupe Bull, a French company heavily subsidized by the French government. Today, HIS does little more than sell upgrades to the creaky old mainframes and minicomputers that it built and sold a decade ago. Honeywell was not the only traditional computer vendor to fall into this kind of a downward spiral. Unisys, Control Data, Wang, and Data General, to name a few, suffered from the same kind of debilitating layoffs.

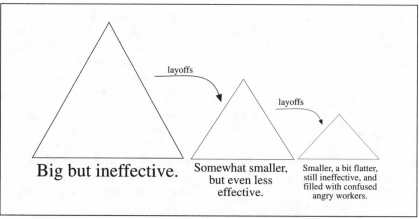

FIGURE 7.1. *Downsizing of Honeywell Information Systems*

Rather than seeing change as something painful, the Electronic Elite embrace it, seeing it as a vehicle for future growth. Carol Bartz, CEO of AutoDesk, commented on this tendency to see change as both positive and inevitable:

> Change management is the toughest thing going these days. It's difficult to reward your organization for stepping out and making the bold move, even if they're wrong. But, remember, any action is better than no action in this industry. I think that the measurement system and the reward system recognizes that, a lot of times, there is no right or wrong answer.

The Electronic Elite encourage their organizations to embrace changes as positive element of their daily work environment.

TABLE 7.1. *Comparison of Pain and Growth Mindset*

CHANGE = PAIN	CHANGE = GROWTH
Product Development. Products are developed slowly, with laborious checkpoints and approvals. Products flow out the pipe slowly, if at all.	*Product Development.* Products are prototyped and developed with great speed. Manufacturing expects changes based on new market conditions and helps with the design process to ensure timely delivery.
Reorganizing. Reorganizing gives the appearance of change without really changing anything. Executives play musical chairs while the corporation falters.	*Reorganizing.* Organizational boundaries are flexible, so reorganizations are uncommon. People join product and service teams that form and disband as needed to get particular tasks done.
Downsizing. By trying to avoid the pain of change, management avoids downsizing until the company is too weak to survive the operation. The layoffs are drawn out over months or even years.	*Downsizing.* Management plans ahead for possible market downturns. If the worst happens, management recognizes failure and quickly makes the cuts that are needed to bring the company back to long-term profitability.

The Change=Growth mindset allows the Electronic Elite to remain flexible at all levels of operation. This makes Electronic Elite organization much more robust, able to run rings around the hidebound organizations of the industrial age, as shown in Table 7.1.

To illustrate the Change=Growth mindset, we'll examine the four strategies that the Electronic Elite implement to help employees embrace change as an inevitable source of renewal and growth. These strategies are:

- Have long-term vision, short-term plans.
- Keep jobs fluid and flexible.
- Make decisions quickly and broadly.
- Hope for the best, prepare for the worst.

STRATEGY 16: HAVE LONG-TERM VISION, SHORT-TERM PLANS

While the electronic elite motivate with a long-term vision (as discussed in the previous chapter) they don't believe in building long-term plans for each and every step along the way to achieving that vision. Simply put, in the fast-moving markets of the Information Age, it's foolhardy to do so. The Electronic Elite, instead, plan in relatively short time frames, often less than a year.

There's nothing inherently wrong with long-range planning, as long as it's directed at markets and opportunities that are stable enough to warrant such commitments. But when markets shift too quickly to nail down, long-range planning can inhibit company growth. Carol Bartz, CEO of AutoDesk, commented:

> You can sit and ponder forever and get lost in what I call "technology purgatory." People do nothing or do something, but too little and too late. If you've only got 7-to 12-month product life cycles and you spend 6 months making a decision, you've missed your window.

Detailed long-range planning is particularly risky when it results in a rigid set of processes for managing changes. The plan, and executing to the plan become more important than satisfying customers or getting products out the door.

Xerox is one company that has suffered from overplanning. The company, although it has an enviable reputation for developing innovative products, is also known for its inability to bring them to market. For example, Xerox pioneered the laser printer, PC networking, and even the graphical user interfaces that make personal computers so easy to use. Other companies, however, have reaped much of the benefits of Xerox's creativity, simply because Xerox suffers from the typical Industrial Age paranoia about change. Computer industry guru Jonathan Seybold commented:

> Xerox had a perennial set of problems. It spends a year or more studying the requirements for a new product. This information is then passed to development, which begins a slow process of bringing the product to market. It has a five-year development cycle, much too slow for such a competitive market. On top of that, if marketing tries to change something along the way, development starts the clock again at the beginning.

Rather than following Xerox's model, Electronic Elite companies implement short-term plans that can be adjusted at a moment's notice to account for shifts in the marketplace. In general, the market for high-tech products is so volatile and competitive that there simply isn't time to ponder all the alternatives before making a decision. People must have a high level of personal and professional flexibility to tolerate the pressure of making frequent and potentially high-risk decisions. Carol Bartz explained:

> I expect to be able to sit down with a manager and have a big "what-if" conversation—this could happen, that could happen. If people can't have that kind of discussion, they're going to be hard pressed to manage in this industry. If people need to really ponder and don't want to express an opinion, then it's harder for me to deal with them.

STRATEGY 17: KEEP JOBS FLUID AND FLEXIBLE

For an organization to be capable of reacting quickly to changes, everybody has to be flexible about job assignments and roles. In the traditional company, job roles and responsibilities are rigid, written down in job descriptions. Often, in these companies, when change is imminent, the first step management takes is to rewrite job descriptions. When market conditions shift, this rather mechanistic approach is usually ineffectual. Case in point was a company that went through a major reorganization every six months, in an effort to respond to a rapidly changing market. Each restructuring included writing detailed job descriptions, defining precise reporting relationships, and assigning goals and objectives for every group. By the time everyone had adjusted to the new hierarchy, the market caused the company to reevaluate it all again.

The Electronic Elite don't apply such snail's-pace tactics to coping with market changes. There just isn't enough time. Bill Campbell, CEO of Intuit, put it this way:

> At Claris, where I was CEO, we didn't reorganize for four years. And we grew substantially during that period, from ground zero to 100 people. Everyone worked together—that was our main principle. People think that you have to reorganize in order to adapt to new markets. They think you have to formally optimize to every little change in the marketplace. But that's bullshit. It makes more sense to leave the organization the way it is. Instead of reorganizing, make sure that management is managing people. Get things done! Don't sit there trying to figure out new ways to organize!

According to the Electronic Elite, rather than concentrating on roles and responsibilities, managers should encourage the organization to be flexible, to do whatever it takes to get the job done. Staff should be able to move from role to role as required, rather than be handcuffed to an outdated job description.

In Electronic Elite organizations, employees are constantly forming and reforming into teams that accomplish the task at hand. Complicated political struggles over who's in what box on the organization chart are unusual. Electronic Elite employees know that everything will be different in a few weeks anyway, so they simply buckle down and do what needs to be done at the moment. Sally Narodick, CEO of Edmark, commented:

> In today's marketplace, you must be able to move very fast and combine the creative talents of many diverse groups of people. You have to be very fluid and not hierarchical. Organizational structures and the job descriptions are constantly in flux. Formerly, we believed that a well-run company had structures and job descriptions clearly defined and written down. I still sometimes feel vaguely guilty that my company doesn't have that, when in fact, it's a strength that we don't have job descriptions and structures. A person's value is not defined by where in the hierarchy he or she is or whether he or she has a window office. People are defined by the creative talent that they bring to a project.

Flexible work hours, too, are important when people must constantly cope with changing conditions. Today's Electronic Elite workers have to stay on top of myriad information sources from all over the world. This requires that they be able to adjust their work hours to meet the needs of an international community. Software venture capitalist Ann Winblad told me:

> There are very few jobs in this industry that are 9 to 5. Strap into your desk in the morning and just react to what you have to do that day. It probably takes most of that day. Add a few meetings to do some early planning, and then your phone system shuts down at 5 and you can get some work done for a couple hours. I would guess that probably the majority of people in this industry work from 9 to 7, that people on average put in 50-, not 40-, hour weeks. That is a fact of life here in this business. There are just so many opportunities and so many challenges that it does take up a lot of time to deal with them.

As you can see, work in Electronic Elite organizations has a very different rhythm, and it demands great personal flexibility. In the Industrial Age you went to work in the morning and left in the late afternoon. You did this Monday to Friday, like clockwork, except for holidays and vacations.

That's not how it works for the Electronic Elite. Their organizations tend to alternate between periods of "crunch"—where lots has to get done—and periods of "slack"—where nothing seems to be happening. During the crunch, the organization goes full bore, with people working around the clock to see that the deadline's reached. Afterward, however, the Electronic Elite expect a period of slack, where it's considered perfectly appropriate to take some "comp time" and goof off. I worked for one organization where the programmers had the habit of taking the afternoon off and going to the cinema together whenever a new *Star Trek* movie came out. Another time I had to reschedule a meeting with Lotus Development Company's marketing group because they had all decided to attend a baseball game in the middle of the work week.

Flexibility also means letting go of the idea that everybody has to be at work at the same time. Electronic Elite employees generally come and go as they please. Because they're goaled on getting things done—not on warming their seats—they're free to be flexible about when they come into the office. Bill Gross, CEO of Knowledge Adventure, commented:

> We have a very flexible work schedule so that people can spend time with their kids, drive the carpool, and so on. As long as people are getting their work done, we don't care.

Electronic Elite proponents believe that work should be an integral part of one's life, not that work is an impediment to "real" life.

STRATEGY 18: MAKE DECISIONS QUICKLY AND BROADLY

A day-to-day commitment to embracing change means that companies must be able to make decisions quickly to take advantage of new opportunities. Traditionally, decision making has been a long, drawn-out affair while information is gathered, distributed, pondered, digested, and commented on. This method certainly worked in other times and other industries, but today, it's suicide. Ann Winblad commented:

> At companies such as General Electric, the methodology required that you write down your strategic assumptions in five or six areas. Then you had monthly or quarterly management reviews where you examined those strategic assumption sets again to see if they were still valid. Today, however, if you wait until once a quarter to review strategic assumptions, you could be out of business.

Decisiveness means processing information quickly, thinking creatively, pressing to a conclusion, and then acting promptly. Decisiveness also means keeping people involved in the decision-making process. The Electronic Elite believe that the people who are going to be affected by a decision, or implement a project that results from a decision, have the right to influence that decision. The Electronic Elite organization still uses debate and discussion prior to making a decision, but this process is not permitted to halt progress. Jonathan Seybold commented:

> The way to get things done is to get consensus among the people who will do the work. The Quakers have a concept called "the sense of the meeting." There are no leaders, per se, and there's never a vote taken. After a discussion of the issues, somebody will say, "I think that the sense of the meeting is . . ." If anyone disagrees with that statement, discussion continues until a consensus is reached. Of course, there are times when I, as a manager, must make a decision that's not acceptable to everybody. However, more often than not, the "sense of the meeting" works quite well. A collective decision makes sense in most cases. Rarely do I go into a meeting with the intent to "sell" them something or with pre-formed opinions. If you approach people with the idea that they are responsible for making the decision, they more readily accept the process and the results of the process.

Decisiveness also means resisting the temptation to fix blame when a decision proves to be the wrong one. The Electronic Elite know that making decisions so quickly means that some of them are bound to be wrong. Safi Qureshey, Chairman of AST Research, explained why:

> I have learned that there is no perfect solution to any business challenge. There are many ways to reach any destination. And, if you are 80 percent, 85 percent, 90 percent right, your hit rate is very good. We cannot wait for the perfect data to flow in and the perfect analysis to be done. The market doesn't behave this way.

STRATEGY 19: HOPE FOR THE BEST, PREPARE FOR THE WORST

Since this quick decision making doesn't always result in success, Electronic Elite organizations can run into problems, especially when they're competing against other Electronic Elite organizations with similar, powerful corporate cultures. When the Electronic Elite are confronted with change that is painful—such as downsizing—they approach it without fear. Mitchell Kertzman, CEO of Powersoft, commented:

> People in any company need to know that layoffs can happen. The job of management is to try to avoid it, but when it is necessary, make certain that it doesn't damage the company beyond repair. You've got to look at every person you hire as a person you might have to lay off. Now we're one of the most successful companies in the business, but we still have to be aware of the downside. We've had an up-and-down history, and I've had to lay people off, as have the other officers in this company. It gives you a sense of how to do it right, once you've gone through it once or twice. What's most important is for the company to recover and reestablish momentum as quickly as possible. Incremental cutbacks are a bad thing.

And because the Electronic Elite aren't frightened of change, they prepare for it from the start. They build their companies with the full knowledge that layoffs might happen. They hope for the best but prepare for the worst. There are three primary ways that the Electronic Elite prepare for the possibility of layoffs, even while they strengthen the viability of their organizations.

First, as already noted, the Electronic Elite look at every person they hire as somebody who might need to be laid off. This means caring about the financial status of the individual who's being hired and making certain that he or she could find employment elsewhere. In most cases, this means hiring the very best people, who, by the nature of their talents and abilities, are the most likely to be able to find other employment in the future.

Second, the Electronic Elite hire the minimum number of people required to do a job. This may seem obvious, but it's often ignored at companies where a Business=Battlefield mindset encourages managers to build armies and empires. The Electronic Elite don't gauge their success on the number of people who work for them.

Finally, the Electronic Elite organize into relatively small, autonomous teams, as we discussed earlier. The product-centered, small-team organizational structure keeps employees and management aware of profitability issues, and creates an early warning system that prompts management to take remedial action before the failure of a particular product causes an undue amount of damage to the corporation at large. Such remedial actions might include shifting resources to get the product back on track, or shifting resources away from the product to ensure greater profitability. This also helps management to cut its losses more quickly and cleanly, rather than causing turmoil throughout the entire organization.

While downsizing is never pleasant, the Electronic Elite's positive attitude toward change helps them to do what needs to be done when it needs to be done. By embracing change, the corporate culture of the Electronic Elite protects their companies, at least to some degree, from the downswings that are part of any dynamic market.

POINTS TO PONDER

Many companies try to change, but find it extraordinarily difficult to do so. Sometimes, the companies that talk the most about change are those that are changing the least. This is sometimes called the law of *inverse relevance*, which might be stated as "the

less you plan to do about something, the more you talk about it."
Keeping this in mind, honestly consider the following questions,
ignoring whatever rhetoric about change might be bounding
around your organization right now.

- How do you personally react to change? Do you like changes
  in your life? Are you committed to your own personal
  growth? How do your personal attitudes about change influence the way that you view the possibility of organizational or
  cultural change?
- Is your organization ready for change? Are people flexible or
  rigid in their job roles? Is there a factory ethic that has everybody working according to set hours on the clock? In today's
  highly interactive world, with remote telephones, fax, and voice
  mail, is it really necessary to have predetermined work hours?
- How quickly do decisions get made in your organization? Can
  people reach agreement quickly or is there a long period of de-
  liberation and negotiation? Are quick decisions made only when
  a manager decides what to do without consulting with employees? What would people in your organization have to believe in
  order to speed the decision-making process?
- Do you have a collection of long-range plans filed away in your
  desk somewhere? If so, how accurate are the plans you made a
  year ago? Two years ago? Five years ago? How much time did
  the long-range planning consume? Were the plans useful for
  guiding day-to-day activities or were they simply needed to get
  funding?
- Has your organization had a layoff lately? If so, do you feel that
  it was handled well? Was there turmoil and lingering pain?
  What could you do, today, to make certain that a layoff isn't
  necessary in the future? And how could you prepare for such a
  layoff at the same time?

Chapter Eight

Redefine Your Current Culture

The first part of this book examined the cultural framework that drives behavior in Electronic Elite corporations. It identified the strategies that, when implemented, result in organizations that are adaptable and flexible and thus better able to compete in fast-moving markets. In some cases, the strategies are not new. For example, forming small, autonomous teams is reminiscent of the cross-functional teams that have been used in business for some time. The difference in the Electronic Elite's approach to teams is that they have internalized the six key mindsets that support the strategy; most other companies have not.

The words "team" and "teamwork" can be interpreted differently. A more traditional manager might seek out employees who are team players, but if the manager believes Management=Control and Employee=Child, a good team player to that manager will be somebody who doesn't make waves, follows orders from management, and doesn't try to change the status quo. The team is assumed to be the corporation itself, replete with all the control mechanisms and bureaucracies that make it so awkward and unwieldy.

By contrast, to the Electronic Elite manager who believes Management=Service and Employee=Peer, a good team player will be somebody who takes the initiative and does whatever it takes to help a small group of like-minded individuals achieve success and renown. The team player in an Electronic Elite organization might even be considered a disruptive factor in a more traditional business environment.

The failure to acknowledge the effects of corporate mindsets is responsible for the many failed attempts to make positive changes within organizations. These failures occur when managers, or management consultants, insist on trying a management technique that isn't supported by the culture of the organization that they're attempting to change. Because the mindset doesn't support the technique, the technique falls flat.

For example, a friend of mine was recently employed at a local aerospace plant. It was a typical traditional "big business" organization; managers were clearly bosses, employees were treated as children. Morale and productivity at the plant were low, so the company hired a management consultant to help turn things around. This consultant convinced the plant manager that he needed to build a better sense of community and "connectedness" between the managers and the workers. This is not a bad idea on the surface. However, because the corporate culture of the organization didn't support the notion of Corporation=Community, this strategy never had a chance.

The plant manager tried to build a feeling of community through such surface activities as a "free hot dog day" at the cafeteria. When the workers were eating their free hot dogs, the plant manager emerged from the executive dining room and visited each table, delivering a prepared speech about the importance of company loyalty. Rather than building a sense of community, this action merely confirmed the workers' opinion that management was patronizing and out-of-touch. The result was a further drop in morale.

Problems occur when a corporate culture can't support the behaviors required to be successful in a given market. Traditional computer vendors of the 1980s and early 1990s are a recent prime example. When they tried to compete with the Electronic Elite, their corporate cultures simply wouldn't support the superfast product development, organizational flexibility, and low-cost structures that were required to compete.

Repeated failure *can* be a positive learning experience for a corporation. Companies can reevaluate their cultures and question the cultural framework on which they've been basing their behavior. This slow process of reevaluation is taking place everywhere in the business world. Today's traditional corporation is different—if only subtly—from the corporation of 100 or even 20 years ago. One of the ways this is apparent, even in the most old-fashioned companies, is in the relationships between managers and workers. They are more casual than they once were, although still formal by Electronic Elite standards.

This corporate evolution often takes place at a geological pace, especially in organizations where the Change=Pain mindset is particularly strong. The inertia generated by this attitude can be almost insurmountable and, unless there is a new foundation for the underlying culture, innovative management strategies simply can't take root. New groundwork must be laid for the attitudes and beliefs that act as touchstones for corporate behavior. The challenge is to accelerate the process of change so that it takes place over a matter of weeks and months rather than years and decades. The potential benefits are immense, and even minor changes can have a far-reaching ripple effect, changing processes and behaviors throughout the entire corporation.

The COMPAQ computer company serves as model for the kind of cultural upheaval that can have a massive positive impact on a company's growth and profitability.

CASE STUDY: THE RENAISSANCE AT COMPAQ

In 1982, a tiny computer start-up called COMPAQ was founded in Texas by a group of engineers from Texas Instruments who had originally sketched out a plan on a cafeteria napkin. COMPAQ's follow-on products were so successful that the company made $111 million in the first year. COMPAQ quickly became the major alternative to IBM as a supplier of personal computers.

COMPAQ also developed a reputation for building the most advanced and most reliable computers in the marketplace. It forged alliances with retail outlets, making it easy for businesspeople to purchase COMPAQ products. It provided telephone support both to the dealers and the customers, so that they could get their computers up and running quickly. COMPAQ beat IBM to the punch with the first computer based on Intel's 386 chip and issued a portable computer long before IBM. By 1988, COMPAQ had become the first company in the world to exceed $2 billion in sales within six years.

By 1990, however, the momentum had shifted. Customer requirements and expectations had changed, and COMPAQ had failed to acknowledge this. Lower-priced, industry-standard PCs had become widely available, but COMPAQ persisted in delivering premium-priced products. Eventually, the company found itself with uncompetitive products, high product costs, a high-margin pricing structure, and high overhead. Further, in a series of moves that baffled industry analysts, COMPAQ invested in technology that had nothing to do with its core market.

COMPAQ's problems reflected its corporate culture, which had been slowly degenerating to resemble the traditional companies to whom it was selling the bulk of its computers. A former employee quoted in *Business Week* (November 2, 1992) summarized the COMPAQ of 1990: "A slickness came into COMPAQ. All of a sudden, if you didn't have an MBA, red suspenders, and these little Gucci slippers, you were nobody." In the words of one industry analyst: "COMPAQ had gone over to the dark side of the force."

Fortunately for COMPAQ and its shareholders, a new leader emerged to revitalize the company. Eckhard Pfeiffer, who had built and run COMPAQ's European organization in the 1980s, perhaps more than any other member of the Electronic Elite had internalized a positive view of change. Here's what he told me about the nature of change in the computer industry:

> Change needs to be constantly on the agenda. We ask everybody: how do we need to do things, not only tomorrow but beyond tomorrow? We've mastered the incredible growth we've had in the last two and a half years with the systems and processes we have, but then outgrew them. We adapt as we move along.

A realist, Eckhard knows that change is the essence of the Information Age:

> This is an industry that has gone through dramatic change and, with all probability, will continue to do so. Ten years go, IBM was leading, and Digital was doing its thing, but the seeds of change had already been planted with the appearance of the personal computer. The speed of change is not just evolutionary; it is revolutionary. It cannot be predicted. Many may take a stab at it and try to predict which way it's going to work out, but the forces are powerful, and the different kinds of industries coming together are creating something entirely new.

In response to what he was witnessing, Eckhard changed the direction of COMPAQ. According to *Business Week* (November 2, 1992), the deciding moment was when Pfeiffer declared that COMPAQ would match the price of any manufacturer in the world. As a premier engineering company that made the "highest of high-tech" PCs, this was a radical statement, running contrary to almost everything that COMPAQ had stood for. Eckhard then set an even more extravagant goal. He announced to his employees—and the world—that COMPAQ could, and would, outsell all other manufacturers of personal computers by 1996.

Eckhard next instructed his executives to cut costs from 35 to 50 percent so that COMPAQ could compete everywhere that people bought personal computers. He knew that if COMPAQ was going to grow, it would have to produce personal computers that appealed to everyone, not just to its corporate consumers of the past. This bold strategy required COMPAQ to alter most of its makeup: manufacturing, marketing, engineering, sales, support.

Previously, COMPAQ's sales force had sold primarily to corporate buyers. Now the base was expanded to include retailers and other distributors that catered to nonbusiness consumers. This required different skill sets, different business contacts, and different ways of deploying sales resources.

Similarly, to manufacture personal computers that had a lower price point (a requirement in the home market) COMPAQ had to find ways to economize on manufacturing without sacrificing overall quality. This required a greater amount of outsourcing of manufacturing to foreign countries, where certain components could be manufactured more cheaply. Again, this required new skills, new business contacts, new ways of deploying manufacturing resources and new ways of managing the flow and supply of parts.

The changes at COMPAQ were just as radical in the area of customer support. The company had to prepare itself for the kind of customer hand-holding that's necessary when selling computers to the general public. The business buyer often has a staff of computer professionals on which to rely for basic support. Not so for Jane and John Q. Public, who must turn to the manufacturer when they encounter difficulties. The cost of providing that level of support had to be factored into the margins for consumer products, thereby exacting even greater demands to keep costs down.

It is difficult to overestimate the impact of these changes on the daily activities of the COMPAQ staff. The company achieved Eckhard's ambitious goal two years early. In 1994, COMPAQ sold more dollars' worth of personal computers than any other company in the world. Eckhard had succeeded in driving massive cultural change at COMPAQ. I'll be drawing on Eckhard's experience as a guide for the practical cultural transformation presented in this and following chapters.

Before proceeding with the strategies for redefining a culture, it's necessary to point out that cultural change need not be something driven from top management. You don't have to be a CEO to make improvements in an organization's culture. A popular expression comes to mind: "Think globally, act locally." Sometimes the best way to create a global corporate culture that's both humane and productive is to create a local pocket of excellence.

This chapter examines four strategies for redefining corporate culture. These strategies are adapted from the processes that the Electronic Elite use when they want to craft or renew their own corporate cultures. They can be applied at a global level to effect a corporate-wide change, or they can be applied locally to create a flexible subculture within a particular group or division. These strategies are:

- Calibrate your current culture.
- Cultivate cultural role models.
- Imagine the possibilities.
- Extend the vision.

STRATEGY 20: CALIBRATE YOUR CURRENT CULTURE

The first step in building a flexible corporate culture is to understand the current state of the corporate culture in which you already are working. This can be difficult to do from the inside, because dysfunctional attitudes and behaviors may be so ingrained that they're difficult to perceive objectively. Nevertheless, it's vitally important to know where you are before you try to get somewhere else. In the words of Eckhard Pfeiffer:

> In hindsight, what worked well was stopping and analyzing the situation and really getting down to the root causes of what didn't work anymore, what we could build our future on, what the important elements were internally as well as externally, and what opportunity we could feel comfortable with. Then we made the big change.

This process of self-examination is not simple. It involves rethinking ideas that many people in the organization may hold dear. To help you through this, I've designed a set of questionnaires that, when answered honestly, can provide a rough estimate of the state of the cultural evolution of your industry, your organization, and yourself. These questionnaires will prompt you to assess your current situation and estimate the level of cultural change that will be required to remain competitive in the future.

The corporate culture of the Electronic Elite, in contrast to traditional corporate culture, is adapted to a set of economic conditions that's come to be known in business jargon as the "Information Age." Economist Michael Rothschild, author of *Bionomics,* writing in *Forbes* magazine (December 7, 1992) sees this transformation in terms of economic evolution:

> The market value of industrial species, such as steel and autos, which dominated the economic landscape of the Machine Age has been overtaken by Information Age species like software and telecommunications. At an ever-accelerating pace, the microprocessor's impact is radically and permanently transforming the economic ecosystem.

The futurist Alvin Toffler, in his groundbreaking work *The Third Wave* saw this change from an industrial to an information economy as being similar to the Industrial Revolution of the eighteenth and nineteenth centuries. The Industrial Revolution transformed a largely rural society—where wealth came primarily from farming the land—into a largely urban society, where wealth came primarily from manufacturing and trade. The information revolution, according to Toffler, is now creating a disintegrated society, where wealth is connected to the control of information.

The value of information reflects itself in fundamental changes in the business models of companies that create new products. Some of the effects that business in an Information Age economy feel can include:

- A sharp decrease in the cost required to manufacture new products through the computerization of manufacturing processes.
- Rapid prototyping of new products through computer-aided design and other automated engineering tools.
- Increased competition from new market entrants, who can use computers to set up businesses quickly and easily.
- Rapid development of new markets with new buyers and new buying habits, such as the sudden growth of electronic commerce taking place on the Internet.
- An increasing number of changes in customer demand, as an increasingly informed consumer base demands more quality for less money.
- Increased restructuring, merger, and/or spin-off activity in the attempt to react to all of the preceding factors.

Questionnaire 1: How Far Has Your Industry Come?

The first questionnaire should be used to define a baseline for your industry, so that you can determine how far it has evolved as an "Information Age" business model. It assesses the amount of change taking place in your industry and the speed with which companies will have to adapt to provide competitive goods and services.

True or False

1. Many of the companies in my industry are undergoing significant organizational change. [ ]
2. My industry couldn't function without a lot of computer power. [ ]
3. We have, or could have, suppliers and customers anywhere in the world. [ ]
4. The time it takes to get a product to market is half what it was 10 years ago. [ ]
5. Outsourcing (hiring outside firms to do inside work) is common in my industry. [ ]
6. The competition generally know what we're doing and vice versa. [ ]
7. A lot of people in my industry communicate through the Internet. [ ]
8. The sheer number of products that my industry covers has recently exploded. [ ]
9. My industry has recently seen the entry of new start-up competitors. [ ]
10. Large companies are buying smaller companies in my industry. [ ]

SCORING: Score 10 for each True answer. Put the result inside the box.

INDUSTRY RATING:

- Industries scoring 80 to 100 are greatly influenced by the In-formation Age and thus are beginning to favor organizations that have cultures similar to that of the Electronic Elite.
- Industries scoring 50 to 70 are somewhat influenced by the In-formation Age. Organizations that can combine Industrial Age techniques with Electronic Elite culture will likely thrive.
- Industries scoring below 50 are still firmly entrenched in the Industrial Age. Until the industry progresses further into the Information Age, the techniques of the Electronic Elite will be of limited usefulness.

Questionnaire 2: Where Does Your Organization Stand?

The second questionnaire assesses the degree to which your current organization has integrated and internalized the cultural mindsets of the Industrial Age. It will give you an idea of how far your organization has been influenced by the business notions of the past and how far it must go to adapt to your industry's current state of evolution.

To calculate your organization's adaptation to the Information Age, rate the importance of these items inside your organization according to the following scale:

1 = extremely important   4 = somewhat important
2 = very important   5 = unimportant
3 = important

Items	Rating (5–1)
Size of offices	[ ]
Job titles	[ ]
Yearly budgets	[ ]
Dress code	[ ]
Chains of command	[ ]
Written job descriptions	[ ]
Corporate image	[ ]

Items	Rating (5–1)
Company regulations	[ ]
Management perks	[ ]
Corporate respect	[ ]
Hierarchy	[ ]
Company politics	[ ]
The "system"	[ ]
The status quo	[ ]
Corporate protocol	[ ]
Playing by the rules	[ ]
Dealing with bureaucracy	[ ]
Regular hours	[ ]
Detailed long-range plans	[ ]
Number of people reporting to managers	[ ]

SCORING: Add up the ratings of these items and put the total in the box.

ORGANIZATIONAL RATING:

- Organizations scoring 80 or above are barely affected by traditional corporate culture and are likely to have been already influenced by Electronic Elite ideas. For these lucky folks, this book can help them hone their culture and become even more productive.
- Organizations scoring from 55 to 75 have many elements of traditional corporate culture, although there are some signs of new productivity and a certain willingness to entertain new ideas.
- Organizations scoring 50 or below are locked into old-fashioned concepts. This can be extremely dangerous for the organization if its industry has evolved. In this case, companies are probably facing a number of fierce and nimble competitors.

Questionnaire 3: Are You Evolving?

The third questionnaire helps you assess your personal level of evolution toward the Electronic Elite model. If you're going to help move your organization in that direction, you'd better know whether you feel comfortable in such a freewheeling environment. The fact that you're reading this book is some indication of your forward thinking. Nevertheless, without realizing it, you may have absorbed aspects of traditional culture that could prove to be a personal impediment to driving the change process.

To measure the extent to which your personality has adapted to the Information Age, answer True or False to the following questions:

1. We would benefit from a more controlled system. [ ]
2. I enjoy developing relationships at work. [ ]
3. I hope to gain more power by changing my organization. [ ]
4. If we didn't have rules, then nothing would get done. [ ]
5. Things would be better if people weren't so stuffy. [ ]
6. It will be easy to influence the culture of my organization. [ ]
7. Winning isn't everything, it's the only thing. [ ]
8. It's a dog-eat-dog world out there. [ ]
9. There's at least one competitor I really hate. [ ]
10. Customers generally aren't certain about what they need. [ ]
11. I say hello to the janitors when I work late. [ ]
12. I like tinkering with organization charts. [ ]
13. Creativity is more important than discipline. [ ]
14. Employees need structure in order to perform optimally. [ ]
15. The best thing about work is the weekends. [ ]
16. I'd like it if people brought their children to work. [ ]
17. I play with computers in my spare time. [ ]
18. I'd rather work for a single boss than be a free agent. [ ]

19. It's important to always show respect for the
corporation. [ ]
20. Position should have its privileges. [ ]

SCORING: Score 5 points for True answers to questions 2, 5, 11, 13, 16, and 17. Score 5 points for False answers to all other questions. Put the total in the box.

PERSONAL RATING:

- If you scored above 70 points, congratulations. You're well suited for Electronic Elite culture and should get along well in the business world of the future. However, you may find it frustrating to work for a company or in an industry that's still enmeshed in traditional thinking.
- If you scored between 50 and 70 points, you're currently undergoing the transition to a set of cultural attitudes appropriate for the Information Age. This book should help crystallize those attitudes and beliefs, which you'll need to foster the kind of success that you want for yourself and for your organization.
- If you scored below 50 points, you're highly influenced by traditional corporate mindsets. However, you're showing an admirable curiosity about the new corporate trends. You may find that it has more to offer than clinging to beliefs and attitudes that worked in the past.

Questionnaire 4: *Who Can You Influence?*

The final questionnaire calculates the influence that you, as an individual, have on your organization. Change of any kind is always driven by a key leader; he or she might be a CEO, a plant manager, or even an outside consultant. Sometimes several people can band together as a sort of group of leaders. The function of the key leader in the corporate change process is to present a vision of the future that gives people a focus on the new structure, and shows how it will enrich their lives while ensuring that the organization will thrive.

It is also important for key leaders to provide a sense of security that will calm people during the inevitable stages of uncertainty when an organization redefines itself. Finally, a key leader must be influential in the culture that he or she is trying to change. This may seem obvious, but before anyone attempts to effect such an impact, he or she has to know how much influence can be brought to bear on the organization. It is that ability to influence that will determine the success—or failure—of any attempt to change a company's direction.

In my experience, most nonmanagement employees underestimate their level of influence, while most managers tend to overestimate their influence. What's important is the degree to which the organization takes social and cultural cues from you as a leader.

To estimate your level of influence in your organization, put a check mark in the appropriate box for the following list of questions:

QUESTIONS	Frequently	Sometimes	Seldom
Do people ask your advice on difficult business questions?	☐	☐	☐
Do people ask your advice on their personal lives?	☐	☐	☐
If you start using a buzzword, do others start using it?	☐	☐	☐
Do you ever organize social events or host parties for your peers?	☐	☐	☐
Are many of the people in the organization your personal friends?	☐	☐	☐
Do people consider you a recognized expert in your field?	☐	☐	☐
Are you generally seen as charismatic and personable?	☐	☐	☐

QUESTIONS	*Frequently*	*Sometimes*	*Seldom*
Are you perceived as a long-term, loyal employee?	☐	☐	☐
Do you feel that your peers really respect your opinion?	☐	☐	☐
Do you respect the opinions of your peers?	☐	☐	☐

SCORING: For every "Frequently" response, score 10; for every "Sometimes" response, score 5; and for every "Seldom" response, score 0. Put the total in the box.

INFLUENCE RATING:

- Scores from 80 to 100 indicate that you enjoy a very high level of influence. People look to you as a role model and as somebody whose opinions and feelings really count. If you attempt to change your organization's local culture, you have a high probability of success.
- Scores from 55 to 75 indicate a moderate level of influence. People value your opinions, but you'll probably need some help from others to effect any meaningful cultural change.
- Scores from 30 to 50 indicate that you're not in a position to attempt to change the culture. The best you can do under these circumstances is to support any cultural change efforts launched by other people in the organization.
- Scores from 0 to 25 indicate that you're working in an environment in which you have little or no cultural influence. You may be doing an excellent job, but people don't look to you for leadership. That's not a problem in and of itself, but it may indicate that you're somewhat disconnected from the rest of the organization.

Assessing Questionnaire Results

Now, take the results of the four questionnaires and put an X on the appropriate line of Figure 8.1.

You are now ready to assess your overall cultural environment. Notice the relative position of your organization's culture to the industry culture. Since most industries are moving toward the Information Age, the best place for an organization to be positioned is about 10 points ahead of its industry's rating. This puts the organization in the enviable position of being the most responsive and most forward-looking organization in the industry. Many organizations are likely to lag behind the evolutionary development of their industry in general. The greater the distance that the organization lags behind the industry, the more likely it is to be having problems.

Next, notice the level of personal evolution that you've achieved. Are you going to be comfortable with the kind of culture that you have to create to make your organization more successful? This number should be at least as high as the level to which you're going to shift your organization's culture; if your current organization is at 50 and needs to move to 70 to become competitive, you should be at 70 yourself to function well in the new culture.

The following are sample charts. Figure 8.2 is a calibration chart from a new CEO who has taken over a small company that manufactures specialty electronic components. The CEO is relatively well-known in the industry and has an engaging personality. This company has been a little behind the times, but he is confident that he can move them back to the front. Coming from

1	10	20	30	40	50	60	70	80	90	100	
—	—	—	—	—	—	—	—	—	—	—	*Industry*
—	—	—	—	—	—	—	—	—	—	—	*Organization*
—	—	—	—	—	—	—	—	—	—	—	*Personal*
—	—	—	—	—	—	—	—	—	—	—	*Influence*

FIGURE 8.1. *Cultural Calibration Chart*

1	10	20	30	40	50	60	70	80	90	100	
—	—	—	—	—	X	—	—	—	—	—	*Industry*
—	—	—	—	X	—	—	—	—	—	—	*Organization*
—	—	—	—	—	—	—	—	X	—	—	*Personal*
—	—	—	—	—	—	—	—	X	—	—	*Influence*

FIGURE 8.2. *Sample Cultural Calibration Chart 1*

an Electronic Elite background, he knows he will be comfortable with the culture that he wants to build.

The sample calibration chart shown in Figure 8.3 was prepared by a marketing manager who wanted to assess whether it made sense for him to stay at his current company and work with the management to drive cultural change, or leave the company for greener pastures.

The marketing manager's company is far behind the rest of the industry in terms of its cultural evolution. The manager's personality, in contrast, is very well-suited to a forward-looking organization, but he has very little influence in his present organization. Given these results, the marketing manager determined that he was too "out of synch" to help his company undergo the cultural change process. He elected to pursue his options elsewhere.

A quick assessment of this sort is no substitute for the kind of corporate soul searching that will be necessary to smoke out the specific problems in any company. In some cases, a strategic consultant who understands corporate cultural issues can help with the process, although relatively few consultants are trained to look at

1	10	20	30	40	50	60	70	80	90	100	
—	—	—	—	—	—	—	X	—	—	—	*Industry*
—	—	—	—	—	X	—	—	—	—	—	*Organization*
—	—	—	—	—	—	—	—	X	—	—	*Personal*
—	—	—	—	X	—	—	—	—	—	—	*Influence*

FIGURE 8.3. *Sample Cultural Calibration Chart 2*

corporate changes as a cultural problem. Remember, some management consultants are as embedded in traditional corporate thinking as the clients they've been hired to help.

STRATEGY 21: CULTIVATE CULTURAL ROLE MODELS

Now we're going to turn our focus outward, to examine some cultural role models. Cultural role models will usually come from your own industry. It's always a good idea to study your major competitors to discover what each does best, then determine the cultural attributes in those organizations that contribute to that successful behavior.

This is not to say that cultural role models *must* be involved in the same industry as you. Looking at the cultures of leading competitors or "best-in-class" companies in other industries enables you to understand what it will take for your organization to succeed. For example, superstores Staples and Office Depot borrowed from the supermarket chains to sell their products—office supplies. The leaders at Staples and Office Depot adapted what worked best at the supermarket chains to their own marketplaces. The clearer a picture of excellence that you can create in people's minds, the easier it will be to convince them to start believing new concepts and behaving in new ways.

Choosing a cultural role model requires market research. First you must determine the essence of the corporate culture that you're trying to emulate. You do this by answering the following questions:

- How do the employees in the model company feel about work? Do they enjoy what they do? Are they having fun? What kind of individuals are attracted to the organization? What kind of individuals stay around for a long time? What kind of individuals move on?
- What do people in the model organization think about business relationships? Does the organization partner easily with other

companies? What is the nature of those partnerships? Do employees feel comfortable listening and talking to customers?

- How do the model's employees feel about profitability? Do they believe they can have an impact on it? Is it tied to the size of their paycheck? If the stock is publicly held, what percentage of the people in the organization own shares?
- What is the nature of control in the model's organization? Who gives the orders? Who follows them? What happens when orders aren't followed? Do managers give orders, or do they give suggestions?
- Why is this model company so successful? What does it do that has been so effective so far? What is the root of that behavior? What would it take to emulate the model's success in your own company?
- What can you learn from this model company? What would it teach you, if it wanted to teach you something? Who does it use as a role model?

Gathering this information can be challenging, especially if the role model is a competitor. In many cases, it will be necessary to hire a market research firm to do the leg work for you. Outside help can also bring a fresh perspective on the cultural change process.

The result of this role modeling process should be a presentation or report that can be distributed throughout your organization. This document not only will prompt your colleagues to think about new ways of doing business but will create the perception that there are better and more effective ways for the organization to behave. Distributing positive information about role model companies helps people visualize the kind of culture they must adopt to compete in the future.

STRATEGY 22: IMAGINE THE POSSIBILITIES

After you've calibrated your culture and identified some role models, the fun begins. You now get to envision a corporate culture that's more flexible, more powerful, and more effective than that of

your competitors. This is a critical element in the process of cultural change, according to COMPAQ CEO Eckhard Pfeiffer:

> We created a new direction and new goals that people could visualize and identify with, and that intuitively sounded right to them. That doesn't mean just going with the majority. It must be right. Then you can communicate it well and get people to "buy in." Then, it's a matter of maintaining the momentum, and making it happen with excitement and good performance—meeting schedules and taking ownership.

To accomplish this calls for some creative visualization. Start with the six cultural mindsets of the Electronic Elite (Chapters 2–7) and use them as a framework for creating a mental picture of what could be different in your organization. Answer the following six questions for each of the six mindsets:

1. How would your people behave if they really believed this?
2. How would your people feel when they came to work in the morning?
3. How would it change your organizational structure?
4. How would it change your compensation schemes?
5. Who would your organization be partnering with?
6. How would this mindset make your company more successful?

Here's how this works. Let's say you're working for a firm that manufactures brass fittings for large commercial construction companies. Your market share is shrinking as the result of foreign competition, which can supply similar products at a lower cost. You know that there's a major opportunity to sell brass fittings to do-it-yourself consumers through mail order and other channels, but to do this, you have to be able to make many different styles of fittings, designs that will change every year. Currently, your organization is set up to make only a few kinds of brass fittings, but in enormous quantities.

Furthermore, you're going to have to find and cultivate new partners to reach this customer. In other words, going after the new market will require substantial cultural change to support shorter product cycles and new business partnerships.

The following is a sample set of questions and answers about the probable effect of the Business=Ecosystem mindset on this brass fitting company. The answers are based on an interview I conducted with a product manager who worked in the organization just described.

1. *How would your people behave if they really believed this?* "There'd be a lot less conflict between individuals and groups. People would get along better. There'd be a lot more cooperation."
2. *How would your people feel when they came to work in the morning?* "I'll bet that they'd be a lot happier to see each other. People wouldn't be so afraid of running into their managers."
3. *How would it change your organizational structure?* "There'd be less need for middle managers, who would then be able to help us find new markets or develop new products. Some of the middle managers are pretty smart, and it's a shame that they're up there just pushing paper."
4. *How would it change your compensation schemes?* "People would be paid based on results rather than on their position in the organization. That's going to be a difficult one for a lot of people to accept."
5. *Who would your organization be partnering with?* "We'd be more comfortable with alternative approaches to doing business. It would be a lot easier for us to locate some new partners to sell our products for us."
6. *How would this mindset make you more successful?* "We'd be better able to tap new markets for our products. New product development wouldn't get tied up in bureaucratic red tape."

Through the process of questioning, we're digging down to the roots of the current culture. We're also visualizing a different way of behaving, a different way of organizing, and a different set of feelings about the work experience. The key is to visualize a culture that automatically takes advantage of opportunities as they occur and that builds a powerful connection among participants.

Once you've answered the questions for each mindset, use the insights to create a statement of what your new culture will be. This statement should be presented in positive terminology, and should have the kind of emotional appeal that's likely to inspire the people in the organization.

The following example of a powerful cultural statement is from Hewlett-Packard. This statement is particularly valuable as a model because HP not only has been successful over many years but has achieved that success by encouraging employees to share HP's cultural vision.

At Hewlett-Packard, we have five underlying organizational values that guide us as we work toward our common objectives:

1. *We have trust and respect for individuals.* We approach each situation with the understanding that people want to do a good job and will do so, given the proper tools and support. We attract highly capable, innovative people and recognize their efforts and contributions to the company. HP people contribute enthusiastically and share in the success that they make possible.

2. *We focus on a high level of achievement and contribution.* Our customers expect HP products and services to be of the highest quality and to provide lasting value. To achieve this, all HP people, but especially managers, must be leaders who generate enthusiasm and respond with extra effort to meet customer needs. Techniques and management practices which are effective today may be outdated in the future. For us to remain at the forefront in all our activities, people should always be looking for new and better ways to do their work.

3. *We conduct our business with uncompromising integrity.* We expect HP people to be open and honest in their dealings to earn the trust and loyalty of others. People at every level are expected to adhere to the highest standards of business ethics and must understand that anything less is totally unacceptable. As a practical matter, ethical conduct cannot be assured by written HP policies and codes; it must be an integral part of the organization, a

deeply ingrained tradition that is passed from one generation of employees to another.

4. *We achieve our common objectives through teamwork.* We recognize that it is only through effective cooperation within and among organizations that we can achieve our goals. Our commitment is to work as a worldwide team to fulfill the expectations of our customers, shareholders, and others who depend on us. The benefits and obligations of doing business are shared among all HP people.

5. *We encourage flexibility and innovation.* We create a work environment that supports the diversity of our people and their ideas. We strive for overall objectives that are clearly stated and agreed upon, and allow people flexibility in working toward goals in ways that they help determine are best for the organization. HP people should personally accept responsibility and be encouraged to upgrade their skills and capabilities through ongoing training and development. This is especially important in a technical business where the rate of progress is rapid and people are expected to adapt to change.

All of this presupposes that you have a very high level of influence inside your organization. In most cases, you'll find it necessary to enlist the aid of your colleagues in order to drive the culture change process. By extending the vision to others, you extend your influence and impact.

STRATEGY 23: EXTEND THE VISION

After you have created the first draft of a culture statement that can drive your organization forward, you need to enlist the support of other key leaders. This is critical, because they will help guide their colleagues and peers through the cultural change process.

The goal is to create a *shared* vision of the ideal corporate culture for your particular organization. To accomplish this, you must work together to create a cultural statement that reflects the best of all your ideas. Note that these leaders need not be managers; in fact, often the most influential people in an organization are those people who are well liked and respected. The term "leader" refers to a person's capability to effect change and help others to accept it; a leader does not necessarily have a managerial title. Former Lotus CEO Jim Manzi put it this way:

> It's insane to think that cultural change can come directly from a top-down structure, or that there's a monopoly on good ideas at the top of the company.

When you find influential individuals in the organization who can't or won't cooperate with the change, it's up to you to help bring them into the fold. Some people can be more difficult than others. With a little patience, however, you'll find that almost anyone can be brought around.

One of the most wonderful human characteristics is the capacity to adapt and change, to use intellect and emotion to create new environments. Even the most conservative corporate bureaucrat would love to find a deeper sense of joy and excitement in his or her work. Given a choice, most people would prefer to work in an atmosphere in which everyone is treated with respect.

Sometimes you must be creative to get a stubborn individual to see the positive aspects of a cultural change.

I recently worked with a very traditional executive whose behavior in the workplace included petty maneuvers, sidelong glances, and a cynical attitude, all common to many traditionally run companies. Rather than write him off as one of the disaffected, I learned through casual chats that his favorite hobby was sailing. He was never happier than when he was riding on the ebb and flow of unpredictable winds, the wind at his back. It was his great escape from a job that he hated, from a style of work that had made him compromise his essential nature, which (unlike his corporate persona) was honest, brave, and straightforward. Thanks to these personal interactions, I felt comfortable bringing up the topic of new work mindsets. I pointed out that doing business in today's fast-moving markets is very much like sailing, that to be successful, he'd have to bring that desire for freedom, of bowing to the winds of change. He began to relax at meetings, to take things lighter.

I've also used presentations, one-on-one discussions, memoranda, electronic mail messages, reports, and videos to promote the value of corporate cultural evolution. Regardless of the media used, be sure that everyone has copies of the material you're advocating. People should be encouraged to discuss the process, and to contribute their own perceptions and opinions. Even if the tenor of the discussions is skeptical, talking helps to break old habits that prevent people from trying new things.

The most important aspect to extending the vision is to invoke a sense of inevitability about this ideal corporate culture. You and your colleagues must communicate that this change not only is required for the continued survival of the organization, it also will enhance everyone's daily work experience. Eckhard Pfeiffer put it this way:

> Ultimately, it's people that make everything happen. That's what we keep saying, but at times we forget it. You have a responsibility to shape the vision of a company, and realize that whatever process you choose will determine the well-being of the organization. You have to drive that vision along with long-term strategies and objectives, and deal with it on a day-to-day basis. And never forget that your competitors are doing the same thing.

In completing this chapter, you've assessed your current culture, created a vision of a new and more flexible culture, and enlisted the assistance of your friends and colleagues in developing a shared vision of the future. Congratulations! The next chapter will help you turn that vision into a reality.

Chapter Nine

Break Limiting
Cultural Patterns

No matter how compelling a vision is, most companies develop inertia. Even people who want and support change will have difficulty breaking old patterns of working and relating to one another. Eckhard Pfeiffer, CEO of COMPAQ, commented:

> Once the organization has become aware of the problems that caused the changes, it takes a while to move on and look for the solutions, for the new ideas, the new direction. It requires a great deal of communication. It does not happen with one memo, at one level of management, or even across two levels of management. It takes a long time to overcome the frustration and the doubts.

There are four major roadblocks to enacting corporate cultural change:

1. *Denial of the Problem.* It's not unusual for individuals and organizations under stress to deny that there's a problem. Companies in denial ignore important market data because the implications of the data, if fully acknowledged, would force the organization to change.
2. *Disbelief in Cultural Change.* People who have worked in traditionally run companies all their lives are likely to be skeptical of

any change process. This is particularly true if they've been exposed to other change methods (reengineering, total quality management, etc.) that have failed because of conflicts with the entrenched culture.

3. *Obsolete Speech Patterns.* The way people use words often is a good indicator of how they approach certain problems. For example, companies that use a lot of military terminology will have trouble escaping from the Business=Battlefield mindset, even if they realize intellectually that the notion is dated.

4. *Outmoded Rules and Practices.* Structures, rules, regulations, guidelines usually must be scrapped and replaced with a new framework on which the new culture can be built. Otherwise, the old foundation will undermine the growth process.

This chapter provides strategies for overcoming each of these roadblocks. To start, though, we'll examine how Wang Laboratories changed its entire corporate culture, creating a new company out of the ashes of failure.

CASE STUDY: THE REBIRTH OF WANG

Wang Laboratories was one of the traditional vendors blindsided by the growth of the personal computer. Like the other traditional vendors, Wang remained in a state of denial for many years about the impact that the personal computer was having on the computer industry.

Wang's decline was the inevitable result of a business culture that was completely inappropriate for the fastest moving industry in the world. Today's computer industry is marked by short product cycles, rapidly declining prices, multiple competing channels, and sudden market shifts. Only companies that can move quickly to exploit new opportunities can survive, let alone prosper and grow. Successful companies have organizations and processes that are flexible and can adapt.

The old Wang was the antithesis of this. Founded by an autocrat, Wang was organized like an imperial court. It suffered from a complex hierarchy of bureaucrats, each striving to protect and control administrative turf. Battles raged between internal factions, as each manager tried to seize political power.

Meanwhile, the computer industry was changing at light speed, leaving Wang's products far behind, and the company began a long and debilitating decline. Layoff followed layoff. Reorganization and downsizing received far more management attention than products and customers. Eventually, the company had no choice but to declare bankruptcy. The stock, once the darling of Wall Street, became almost worthless.

This change in fortune took a tremendous toll on the engineers, marketers, salespeople and clerical staff who were the foundation of the corporation. Many of the most talented left for other companies. Those that remained harbored extraordinary anger at Wang's management, whose infighting and lack of vision had driven a great corporation into financial disgrace.

However, Wang had one thing going for it—it had "bottomed out." The remaining Wang employees—collectively and individually—knew that *something* had to change.

Today, Wang is a completely different company; it is a *software* company. In a certain sense, this was always the case. It was Wang's excellent word processing software that had made Wang's stand-alone word processing systems so popular, and Wang had a tradition of creating innovative software for office workers. Essentially, the pain of bankruptcy allowed Wang to realize its true identity. The company issued new stock and found new investors. Wang transformed itself from a near-dead hardware vendor into an interesting software company that's positioned for growth.

One of the leaders key to this amazing turnaround was Dan Cerutti, whom I've quoted earlier. Dan has been something of a professional iconoclast throughout most of his career. At IBM, where he was in charge of the software for IBM's high-powered workstations, he was a vocal and visible opponent of IBM's dress code, and bucked convention by wearing blue jeans when he met with IBM's customers. Dan left IBM to fill the software VP slot at

Wang where he played a crucial role in the cultural change process. Dan then left Wang to start his own software company, Amulet, which is building software for the Internet.

I caught up with Dan when he was still software VP at Wang, deep in the thick of Wang's cultural transformation. Dan told me about how he and his colleagues were changing the company:

> We created a cultural revolution at Wang. I don't think that [former CEO] Miller really understood how serious those changes had to be. The people here now are new age information thinkers, and share the same desire for a new Wang. I'm the extreme, and I'm the first to admit it. I brought with me the objective to literally reengineer the culture.

Dan, along with the rest of the management team, painted a picture of a renewed company that resembled Microsoft more than it did the hardware company it once had been. This vision inspired the remaining employees and was momentous enough to bring new talent to the company. Investors got on the bandwagon. At one point, two venture capitalist firms were bidding to give $55 million to get the new company launched. Employees received special founder's stock, thus making the prospect of staying with or joining Wang potentially lucrative.

Wang's management found ways to shake the organization out of its complacency. New staff brought experience to help propel the new direction. Dan Cerutti commented:

> We had to bring in new blood. Not too much, though. A third is about the most any team can absorb, in my experience. Fifty percent is too disruptive. Think about that—for every three people, two have historical continuity. That turns out to be just right.

Wang's management also dismantled the elaborate web of executive privileges and perks that made regular employees feel like second-class citizens. For example, the executive elevator, an express to the headquarters' top-floor executive suite, was converted into a regular elevator. Wang's management also planned events to symbolize the new Wang. Dan Cerutti gave me this example:

We had a day out in the parking lot, like a celebration. We had a dunk tank, and the people who were dunked were the senior people. The employees loved it. They gathered around to throw balls at the bosses and put them in the water. It was a great thing to do that wouldn't have been possible in the old days.

The way that people treated one another changed, too. Dan Cerutti again:

Just as significant as the dramatic moves are the little ways you treat people every day. When you stop by people's offices, you just treat them with respect for what they bring to the business. In response, they respect your right to make a decision, your obligation to make a decision.

Wang's journey from being the biggest disaster in the computer industry to (in the words of one analyst) becoming "a billion-dollar start-up" proves that massive corporate cultural change not only is possible, but practical. If Wang, bankrupt and in decline, can rework itself, then any organization can do it.

The Wang experience suggests four strategies to overcoming roadblocks to swift cultural change.

ROADBLOCK	STRATEGY
Denial of the problems	Directly confront denial
Disbelief in cultural change	Sacrifice the sacred cows
Obsolete speech patterns	Transform the vocabulary
Outmoded rules and practices	Reinforce the new culture

STRATEGY 24: DIRECTLY CONFRONT DENIAL

As stated already, one of the most powerful negative forces is denying the problems. When a company is in denial, it precludes an accurate evaluation of the facts. Eckhard Pfeiffer, CEO of COMPAQ, commented:

You have to stop the denial process, which is hard because it's not something intentional. It is a mindset. Therefore, I test it every day. I'm always asking: Are we in a state of denial in any of our activities? Are we doing things just because we've always done it that way? You have to be willing to come to the conclusion that you might not have the right strategy, might not have the right product, might not have the right cost, might not have the right distribution concept, or the right alliances, or the right technology.

Good examples of debilitating corporate denial are the American automobile manufacturers. How long did it take them to act on consumer demand for reliable cars that didn't guzzle gas? Ten years? Fifteen years? And let us not forget IBM. Big Blue took its first big loss in 1991. At that time, CEO John Akers characterized the problem as a "difficult economy," even though companies such as Microsoft and Intel were posting gigantic growth and profits that same year. IBM had to lose $15 billion over three years before management admitted that something was wrong with IBM, not with the economy. That's a pricey wake-up call, and could have been avoided if IBM's management had confronted reality from the start.

Companies that have a long tradition of success often have the most difficulty acknowledging that what used to work no longer does. Too often, as in the case of IBM, change has to be forced on them. It takes major losses, massive layoffs, and even bankruptcy before most companies begin to come to grips with the need for change. And by then, it may be too late. COMPAQ CEO Eckhard Pfeiffer comments on anticipating change:

It's easier to get it done [effect change] when you are in a state of crisis. The real challenge comes when you are steaming right along and everybody is preoccupied with getting the job done and you have to ask, are they still keeping their eyes and ears open for the changes that come very rapidly in this industry? Are they looking to the next design cycle or the one beyond that?

Digital in the early 1990s is another good example of the high cost of denial. The overwhelming market evidence indicated that decentralized companies with autonomous product-focused teams (such as Microsoft, HP, Novell) were more effective than centralized, monolithic companies (including IBM and Digital). Despite this, the first major action that Digital CEO Bob Palmer took when he assumed office was to centralize Digital further still, organizing it around broad industry categories, thus strengthening the power of the bureaucracy at corporate headquarters. This seemed to accelerate Digital's decline rather than help it become profitable.

By 1995, Digital had changed its philosophy somewhat. Rather than centralizing like in the old days, Digital was becoming a looser confederation of divisions addressing different market segments. In essence, Digital has been trying to emulate the autonomous divisional structure that was working so well at Hewlett-Packard. As you might expect, Digital's financial problems began to ease and it became profitable again. This change in direction, however, was accomplished only with great effort because much of Digital's culture valued centralized control and was in denial that Digital's centralization was a liability.

So how do you break an organization out of denial? An organization—its employees—must confront its situation. One way to do this is to prepare an honest, detailed report or presentation on the consistent failures of the organization and map those failures to the current culture. This clarifies the all-essential point that continued failure is inevitable unless the culture changes.

As with the cultural vision statement described earlier, this confrontation presentation must be "owned" by more than one person. This is important because when only one leader or influencer points out problems, the tendency of the organization is to blame the messenger. By enlisting multiple leaders and influencers in the process, the focus is directed away from personalities and on the actual problems.

To execute this strategy, list the failures that the organization has experienced over the past three years. Then, for each failure, write down the aspect of your current culture that contributed to the failure. Here are some examples:

- We failed three times to form a partnership with a critical channel. Cause of failure: Our bureaucracy couldn't move quickly enough to approve the agreement because people were afraid of making a bad decision.

- We didn't get a critical product out on schedule or on budget. Cause of failure: Every time that we had to make midstream corrections, we had to write complicated justifications and obtain multiple management approvals.
- Our division keeps losing money because we can't reduce overhead or increase sales. Cause of failure: We aren't exploring new opportunities because our approach to both manufacturing and sales is unimaginative and regimented.

Using the insights that you've gained through this process, create a presentation that illustrates the direct connection between your current culture and the failures that the organization has experienced. Refine this presentation by working with your friends and colleagues who are participating in the cultural change process. Then roll the presentation into the rest of the organization, as described next.

As you and your team prepare to present this material to your co-workers, remember that you're dealing with emotions. You're asking people to think in new ways, to evaluate business events differently, and to act congruently with those revisions. This may be difficult for some, especially those who are convinced that Change=Pain. In general, people aren't going to appreciate their failings being pointed out; it's much easier to pretend that nothing is wrong. But that's exactly what you can't allow to happen. Based on my own experience, there are three important rules to follow when you're confronting denial:

1. *Don't Get Personal.* Make certain that everyone understands that the problem hasn't been caused by a particular individual, but by the endemic *culture* and the *behaviors*. This will reduce the level of fear and make the organization more receptive.
2. *Keep It Light.* Use humor to lighten the situation. Use cartoons to help get your points across. The more that people associate fun with the change process, the more likely they'll be to embrace it.
3. *Point the Way.* Provide alternatives to the current—unsuccessful—way of doing business. Establish the direction that you

want the organization's culture to move. Your objective isn't to make people feel bad, but to get them to think positively about the changes you're proposing.

Recently, I helped a high-tech company launch a campaign to publicize its entry into a new product category. This normally wouldn't have been very difficult—standard marketing stuff—but the organization was highly controlled, run by an iron-hand director, who held all the power. As a result, the managers below the director were afraid to make any decisions.

To complicate matters, everyone in the organization reported to more than one manager. This "matrix management" was supposed to foster teamwork, but its result was to disperse responsibility so that nobody "owned" anything, thus nobody could be blamed when something went wrong. Under these circumstances, few people were willing to stick their necks out to do real work.

Needless to say, this was not the ideal situation in which to create an effective environment for marketing new products, an activity which demands energy and adaptability. It was my charter to mold a section of this constricted organization into something resembling a marketing powerhouse. The first challenge was to get the marketing team to understand that business as usual wouldn't work in this case. This meant encouraging them to confront the way they were doing business. I researched the history of the organization and identified multiple instances where the organization had failed to accomplish tasks similar to the one at hand.

I then made a slide detailing these failures. Finally, I asked the marketing team three questions.

1. What do you think will happen if we do the same things again?
2. Why not try something different?
3. What have we got to lose?

Notice that I did not have to get into complicated cultural issues. All I had to do was to create a connection between the status quo and failure. The three questions set up the possibility of a new set of behaviors so that the group could start visualizing a more positive approach.

When I presented this slide, a number of people had a very emotional answer to the final question, "What have we got to lose?" In fact, many people in the organization were afraid of losing their jobs if they didn't follow all the rules, even though those rules invited failure. I therefore created another slide, which I entitled "What This Team Is All About." This slide stated three principles that we were going to use to evaluate everything that we did:

1. We're going to launch a world-class effort.
2. We're going to advance our careers by trying new things.
3. We're going to have a lot of fun.

Again, I didn't make it complicated. The "advance our careers" principle turned the tables on the fear of job loss by making it clear that everyone's long-term employability depended on achieving new skills, which could only be accomplished if the team members were willing to try new things.

This simple, two-slide presentation confronted the organization's denial while simultaneously suggesting a better and possibly more successful way to behave. In the end, the marketing campaign was the most effective that the organization had ever attempted. It won a corporate marketing award and advanced the careers of the team members who took advantage of the opportunity to learn new skills. This story also illustrates that it doesn't have to be a high-powered CEO who creates a cultural change. It can happen from the grass roots, too.

STRATEGY 25: SACRIFICE THE SACRED COWS

Old habits die hard. Even if an organization is fired up with the possibility of a new culture and is willing to confront the reality of its past failures, some people will continue to behave in obsolete ways. I call these habitual behaviors "sacred cows" because, like the sacred cows of India, they are immune from criticism or opposition.

For example, one of Wang Laboratories' sacred cows was the expected deference shown to management, a holdover from its original, highly autocratic corporate culture. As described earlier, in a symbolic debunking of this practice, employees unceremoniously dunked managers in a tank of water at a company picnic.

There has to be an "in your face" quality to sacrificing a sacred cow. Otherwise, it doesn't serve to interrupt the patterns of behavior in a sufficiently dramatic way. It has to be an act that simultaneously buries the old culture and establishes the new one. To illustrate this, the following true story shows how a single individual can have a major effect on an entire culture.

These events took place at a software development center that was located far from the corporate headquarters of a mainframe manufacturer. About 100 programmers had been working night and day on a very complicated piece of software. Suddenly, top management decided to assign a new director to the center, someone who had been trained at corporate headquarters.

The announcement couldn't have been made at a worse time. There had always been a certain amount of tension between the development center, which was full of counter-culture types, and corporate headquarters, which was strictly old school. As a result of this announcement, rumors began to surface that "the development center will be shut down," "the project's going to get canceled," "they'll make everyone wear a tie" and so forth.

One senior programmer quit, and made certain that everyone knew he was taking this action because he disapproved of the change in management. This created even more rumors, more uncertainty. The ambitious deadline was forgotten and work on the software project ground to a halt. A delegation from corporate headquarters were scheduled to visit the development center, to officially hand the reins of power over to the new director. It was, in the minds of the programming staff, the beginning of the end.

One programmer, however, wasn't unsettled by all this organizational brouhaha. He was the project leader, the person responsible for ensuring that the software project was completed on time. From his perspective, the identity of the new director had little to do with getting the software out on time and satisfying the customers who were waiting for delivery. He tried to convince his co-workers that they should continue to work, but to no avail.

Out of frustration, the project leader rented a gorilla costume—a hairy black bodysuit with black rubber hands and feet—and brought it to work on the day that the corporate delegation was scheduled to arrive. He waited until the executives were comfortably settled in the conference room. Then he put on the gorilla suit, and emerged from the bathroom in all his hairy glory. He sped through the hallways, ignoring the gasps of his co-workers and the shriek of a secretary who wandered into his path, and went straight to the conference room, opened the door, and entered.

Twelve executives stared up at him, mouths agape. Growling and huffing, he stumped and shambled around the conference room table doing a fine imitation of a disgruntled gorilla. Then he left without a word, returned to his office, and changed back into his normal T-shirt and blue jeans.

Three things happened as a result of this incident. First, the programmers forgot all about the corporate shake-up and, laughing, returned to work. Second, the new director realized that he wasn't going to be able to manage this group the same way he had managed his group at headquarters. Third, the delegation from corporate headquarters decided that it would be best if they left the development center alone in the future.

The project leader's act became the stuff of legend. With this one dramatic action, the project leader had ensured that the software was released on time, a goal that was, after all, far more critical than a change on an organization chart.

Of equal importance, the gorilla incident changed the culture of that development center by sacrificing a sacred cow that exists inside many organizations—the notion that politics, not products, are important to success. I'm not suggesting everybody go out and rent gorilla suits. But I am pointing out that individuals have the ability to change an organization's culture. It requires courage and the willingness to take bold, dramatic action.

Sacrificing a sacred cow works best when it has a certain element of humor in it. For example, I was once in an organization where it was common for people to get heated and angry during meetings. This usually caused the meeting to degenerate into circular arguments and pointless blaming. This habit was a sacred cow that consumed an extraordinary amount of the participants' energy without providing any noticeable benefit.

It was clear to me that we needed to sacrifice this sacred cow if the team was to become more effective. At the next meeting, I waited until the discussion began to heat up, and then I pulled out a PEZ dispenser. (PEZ is a candy that comes in a small plastic tube with a cartoon head attached to its top. This one had Wonder Woman's head on it.) Quietly, and without comment, I tipped back the head of the PEZ dispenser and ate a piece of PEZ. I then returned it to my pocket.

This action was so weird and so out of place that the people in the meeting lost track of their anger. They returned to their discussion but in a much lighter frame of mind. Presently, the conversation began to heat up again. Out came the PEZ dispenser, but this time, I held it out to the person next to me and asked (in a very serious voice): "Would *you* like a PEZ?" A couple of people laughed and the meeting continued. By this time, the entire atmosphere of the meeting had changed. People kept looking my way to see if I was going to pull out the PEZ again. The next time it heated up, I took the PEZ dispenser out, and handed it around the room, saying "I think we could all use a PEZ right about now." The PEZ dispenser went the rounds, the managers grinning sheepishly as they popped little tart candies into their mouths.

From that time on, all I had to do was take out the PEZ dispenser and people would start to smile. It became a defining metaphor for the team and kept everyone focused on having fun, rather than losing tempers. A minor victory, perhaps, but one that changed the organization's culture, making it more productive.

Sacrificing sacred cows is also more of an art than a science. First you must identify the sacred cows. Then you design a dramatic way to sacrifice each one publicly, so that people can internalize the emotional message of the sacrifice. The specific form of the sacrifice will vary according to the circumstance of the organization and the nature of the sacred cows, but with a little creativity, this strategy can be an effective vehicle for accelerating cultural change.

STRATEGY 26: TRANSFORM THE VOCABULARY

Every organization and industry has buzzwords used in conversations, meetings, and memoranda. These words both reflect and strengthen the corporate culture that encourages their use.

At Digital in the 1980s, for instance, a visit to a customer site was known as "talking to the customer." A marketing manager at Digital might complain that his or her people weren't spending enough time "going on the road and talking to customers." Attending a trade show was a good opportunity "to get in front of a lot of customers and talk to them about our products." This phrase contained hidden information about Digital's culture. When Digital representatives visited customers, they always did the talking; they almost never *listened*. Thus the phrase "talking to the customer" reflected a certain arrogance that had developed at Digital.

You can discern a world of information about the internal thought processes of a company merely by listening closely for the words that come up frequently in a typical business meeting. As soon as I hear a manager refer to his or her employees as "troops," I know immediately that he or she—and probably the rest of the organization—is caught up in the Business=Battlefield mindset. The same is true of Electronic Elite mindsets. When I hear people in a meeting discussing "market niches" and "growing a business" and "harvesting investment," it's usually an organization that resonates to the Business=Ecosystem mindset.

Terminology isn't just a reflection of culture; constantly repeated, it reinforces the culture making the culture more concrete. Every time an executive uses terms such as "control the business" and "control the situation," he or she is sending a subliminal signal that makes the Management=Control mindset more influential.

Thus, when you encourage the use of a vocabulary that reinforces a new culture and discourages the old one, you're invoking change on a regular, very intimate basis.

One method that is effective for doing this is what I call a *vocabulary poster*. The purpose is to identify the words and phrases that reinforce the old culture and to suggest replacement words and phrases that reinforce the new culture. For example:

FAILURE WORDS	SUCCESS WORDS
Talking to customers	Listening to customers
Fighting the good fight	Striving for excellence
Working the system	Serving the customers

At one Fortune 100 company, I created a one-page vocabulary poster, consisting of about 10 transformations, and handed out copies at a small meeting. Without my having to do anything else, the poster was recopied and, within two weeks, was in offices throughout the company, including the office of the CEO.

Another way to use a vocabulary poster is to give a copy to everyone in the organization and request that no one use the failure words for 10 days. You'll be surprised at how effective this can be. Each time somebody stops him-or herself from saying one of the failure words, it trains the mind to think in new ways. And each time somebody uses a success word, it helps to lock a newer, more positive culture into place.

However, success words can lose their original meaning through misuse or overuse. I worked with one company where the new CEO told employees that he wanted them to be "customer-focused." As a result, subsequent presentations at all levels of the corporation were immediately plastered with references to the "customer." At one presentation where the word "customer" was used on almost every slide, I finally asked what the presenter meant by the term. It turned out that the "customer" in this case was the presenter's own corporate headquarters. To this individual, being "customer-focused" had been warped into "focusing on corporate politics." The presenter had latched onto the buzzword, but ignored the essence.

A new vocabulary *must* be an external representation of *real cultural change*, not a patina of buzzwords that covers up the status quo. Then the use of a success-oriented vocabulary, when coupled with other strategies, can greatly accelerate the change process.

Strategy 27: Reinforce the New Culture

Any attempt to improve an organization's culture is destined to fail if the processes at work in the organization continue to reinforce the old culture. The cultural transformation discussed can provide the conceptual framework for a new culture, but without *action*, the old culture will remain in place. You have to be ruthless about weeding out old behaviors, rules, structures, standard operating procedures, bureaucracies, and other elements of the old culture. Dan Cerutti, former Wang vice president, commented on the need to continually question old ways:

> Every day, you have to teach people a different way to do business. It means questioning. I question everything. Somebody comes in with some process and says, "We need to do this." I just ask, "Why?" If the answer is something like, "Because that's the way we do things here," it's generally something that's only a waste of time. If it can't pass the "why" test, then it's probably work that can be eliminated. In other words, people may have lost track of why they are doing something, although there might have been a very good reason 10, 15 years ago.

Overachieving to the new culture means tirelessly promoting and encouraging behaviors that reinforce the new culture. Here's the advice of Mike Maples, former executive vice president at Microsoft, offered this advice for achieving a more powerful corporate culture:

> Corporate culture allows you to move in a direction. It's the belief system that people filter their actions through. In order to change the way a company reacts or behaves, you really have to change the corporate culture. In most cases, companies tend to move from a more freeform to a more structured organization.

The entrepreneurs start it, but the venture capitalists or the stockholders replace the management with somebody who's more control-oriented and more process-oriented. So you're continually marching toward more control and more process. If you're going to perform a cultural transplant in a company, that's what you've got to reverse. You've got to decide what the cultural behaviors are that you stand for. If I had a company and was tasked with changing the culture, I would make sure that I understood exactly the current culture. I would communicate thoroughly to the employees what part of the culture we were keeping and what part we were changing and what we were changing it to. Then I'd go overboard in reinforcing the culture that we wanted to move to. Any time there was a borderline decision or a borderline process, I'd overachieve to the new culture.

How do you do this? The answer is simple, because if you've read the book this far, you already know how to do it. The way that you overachieve to the new culture is to go through the strategies in this book and implement them as quickly and as thoroughly as possible. This may prove easier than you think. After all, you've already conditioned your organization to look forward to a new culture. People will be waiting to see if this "cultural change stuff" is just more talk. When you actually start implementing the strategies, people will welcome the intent to make the vision of cultural change into a day-to-day reality.

At the completion of this chapter, you've learned how to break through the roadblocks that keep the new culture from being adopted across the organization. You've also learned how to implement the practical strategies based on that culture. In Chapter 10, you'll learn how the Electronic Elite harness electronic mail to strengthen their corporate cultures, making them even more powerful and responsive. We'll also learn why electronic mail can be dangerous to companies that are still enmeshed in traditional business behaviors.

Chapter Ten

Harness Electronic Mail

One of the most important technologies transforming the business world today is electronic mail. Electronic mail and the computer networks that support it are among the fastest-growing segments of the computer industry. Tens of thousands of corporations are wiring their desktops together so that people can swap memos at light speed. The business world also is making use of the Internet, which lets businesses connect their internal electronic mail systems together. Already it's possible in many companies to send electronic messages to business contacts around the world.

Electronic mail has an enormous potential to help companies become more productive. Communicating and coordinating the activities of many different people can be difficult, even with a telephone. This is especially true today, when business travel and voice mail seem to guarantee that you never *actually* talk with the person you're trying to reach. Unlike voice mail, you can use electronic mail to send people long documents, chock-full of interesting information. A few minutes and—blip!—the document is on the recipient's desktop computer.

Of course, you could always send a fax, but electronic mail is cleaner, faster, and less expensive. Suppose you have to provide information to 50 people. With electronic mail, you can send everyone a copy in a matter of a few seconds. Faxing might take hours of dialing and redialing.

Because of the obvious benefits, companies often use electronic mail to make them more productive. Even traditional organizations have jumped on the electronic mail bandwagon. It's commonly believed that electronic mail can make any company, even a monolithic, traditional company, more responsive, flexible, and productive. We'll explore whether this is necessarily true in a moment.

The idea that electronic mail will be a productivity panacea is certainly nothing new. In 1970, an influential book titled *The Office of the Future*, written by computer scientists Uhlig, Farber, and Bair, described a number of technologies that were under development in academic laboratories. One of these technologies was electronic mail. The book was enthusiastic about the effect that this new technology would have on the business world. According to the authors, it would provide "overwhelming advantages" and have a "very positive impact." It was predicted that, using it, people would make fewer errors and thus produce higher-quality work. The book went on to anticipate an acceleration in critical business processes, more flexible work hours, and an increase in the availability of important information, all of which would result in greater job satisfaction. In short, the authors predicted that electronic mail would be instrumental in the evolution of more productive and humane work environments.

The next few years saw the technological predictions of *The Office of the Future* turn into a commercial reality. By 1980, most of the traditional mainframe and minicomputer vendors had corporatewide electronic mail and were beginning to hawk these products to their customers. The microprocessor revolution then made electronic mail available on low-cost Intel-based desktops and servers. At the same time, the U.S. government began developing the Arpanet, the network that eventually grew into today's Internet. It's time we asked ourselves: How valid are the predictions that *The Office of the Future* made over 25 years ago? Does electronic mail automatically make all companies more productive? Let's explore these questions in another case study.

Case Study: Electronic Mail and Traditional Computer Vendors

It was 1992, and I was at an office automation conference. On the discussion panel were representatives of IBM, Digital, and Wang—the three traditional industry leaders in corporate-wide electronic mail. All three had been selling electronic mail for over a decade. Although PC-based mail products like cc:Mail from Lotus were eating away at the edges of their market share, all three companies had solid customer bases.

The guys on the panel were carefully dressed in impeccable wool suits, as alike as three peas in a pod. Their presentations were the same as well. All three agreed that electronic mail would inevitably make companies more productive. The promises were familiar:

"Executives will be better informed."

"Managers and employees will communicate more quickly."

"Tedious paperwork will be eliminated."

"Vast sums of money will be saved."

The audience consisted mostly of conservatively dressed computer professionals who had built their careers selling the benefits of IBM, Digital, and Wang equipment inside their own companies.

Presently, the session moderator asked for questions from the floor. A few audience members raised their hands, seeking clarifications of minor points. Then silence—the respectful kind of silence that often happens at the end of a successful, if uncontroversial, conference session. The moderator was about to close the session, when a young man in the back of the room raised his hand. I have to admit that he looked a little out of place at the conference, for he was dressed in jeans, T-shirt and high-top tennis shoes.

"I have a couple of questions," he said.

The man from IBM smiled indulgently. "Let's have them, son."

"Do you use your own products?"

The man from IBM glanced at his fellow panel members, who nodded. "Why, of course. We wouldn't ask our customers to buy something that we didn't use ourselves."

The young man in the audience scratched his head. "Well, if electronic mail is so great and can make employees so productive and give them such a 'competitive advantage,' how come IBM, Digital, and Wang revenues are all going down the toilet?" Remember, this was in 1992, and all three companies were in deep financial trouble.

The guys on the panel looked as if they had been slapped in the face. The audience shuffled in discomfort. After all, nobody likes to hear that the emperor has no clothes, especially if you've been buying from the same tailor. The Digital guy muttered a lame joke about becoming "unintentionally nonprofit," but it was too late. The atmosphere of self-satisfied chumminess had disappeared. When the moderator closed the session, people left the room muttering to themselves and avoiding the young man who had asked the offending question.

And yet, the question was a valid one. For years, the traditional mainframe and minicomputer vendors had been claiming that electronic mail made companies more competitive, better able to adapt to rapid market changes. And they had been using their own technology for years. Unfortunately, technology by itself isn't enough.

Unless the corporate culture is ready for the new technology, productivity gains are likely to prove elusive. In fact, the combination of electronic mail and traditional business culture, far from making traditional businesses more effective, can even make them less effective than before. Let's look at Wang Laboratories first. Wang was an early pioneer in electronic mail, both in selling it to customers and using it in-house. Despite Wang's long experience with the technology, however, the organization didn't use electronic mail very effectively, according to former Wang employee Ann Palermo, who was recently the groupware vice president at International Data Corporation, one of the largest computer market research firms in the world:

> I don't know if electronic mail makes companies more efficient. It's really just an alternative means of communicating. For example, at Wang, there was a formal protocol for electronic mail. If you sent something a few levels above your own, you had to copy

everybody in between. There wasn't the free flow of information that everybody anticipates with electronic mail. It was very political. You had to be careful how you worded things and what kinds of issues you raised. It was like memo writing, only quicker. It created a lot more fire drills, a lot more panics about one thing or another—a lot of running around.

Electronic mail at (the old) Wang did make communications faster. The management, however, tried to use this improved communication to gain greater control over employee behavior. This increased the number of orders from headquarters, as well as the number of requests for status reports. Wang employees began to focus more on internal issues rather than building products that customers wanted. Wang's electronic mail system was used as a mechanism to oversee, to check on progress, to intrude on the day-to-day doings of the regular employees.

Prior to the installation of electronic mail at Wang, there was a balance—albeit an uneasy one—of power between headquarters, the engineers, marketers, and salespeople. Electronic mail put power firmly at Wang headquarters. This weakened Wang by making it *more* centralized and thus *less* able to react to market changes. While many factors were contributing to Wang's decreasing fortunes, electronic mail—rather than acting as a productivity panacea—was actually making things worse.

The danger with electronic mail is that it can create a corporate cyberspace where managers have so much immediate access to information that they want to micromanage everything. Rather than being used as a tool for coordinating activities, the electronic mail system can degenerate into a means to centralize control of an organization, thus extracting individual initiative. Electronic mail, in the hands of a manager who's internalized the Corporation=Machine mindset is all too likely to use the system to make his or her organization more machinelike.

In the 1980s, electronic became the tool IBM's corporate bureaucrats needed to guarantee that nothing was done without their prior approval. This made it increasingly difficult for the company to launch new products, while simultaneously reinforcing the status quo. A former IBM vice president had this to say about the way electronic mail was used at IBM:

> E-mail was designed to facilitate, but what it did was make people prisoners of the system. For the sake of the efficiency, a lot of procedures have been automated. But people seldom ask: "Why am I doing this procedure?" Procedures that are automated become almost impossible to change. They think they're so clever for automating all this stuff but it's really an albatross around their neck.

The main peril is that the corporate bureaucracy will actually use the system to get "control" of the company. In that case, something very curious is likely to happen. Rather than using the electronic mail system to increase the speed with which the bureaucracy grants approval, the bureaucracy uses the electronic mail system to require approval for an increasing number of employee activities. Giving electronic mail to bureaucrats simply serves to empower the bureaucrats, making organizations more bureaucratic and therefore less productive. Powersoft CEO Mitchell Kertzman commented:

> Most organizations use electronic technologies as a modernization of their existing communication methods and human interactions, rather than using them to significantly change things.

The more powerful the technology and the greater the potential benefit, the greater the potential for abuse. With electronic mail, a well-run organization will become better run, because information will flow faster. A poorly run organization, on the other hand, will simply become even more dysfunctional.

Case in point: Digital Equipment Corporation in the late 1970s and early 1980s. According to authors Glenn Rifkin and George Harrar (in their excellent 1988 book, *The Ultimate Entrepreneur*), Digital at that time was a hotbed of internal politics, with much of the backbiting and intrigue conducted via electronic mail. According to one product line manager, "you had to read your mail *before* you went to work because they would send copies to everybody and maybe a thousand people would see some cheap shot before you even got to the office." This misuse of electronic mail put extraordinary stress on the company's key leaders. At least one manager felt obligated to wake up at 4 A.M., just to keep tabs on the political situation. According to authors Rifkin and Harrar, electronic mail became a convenient way to spread those two hallmarks of the predatory bureaucrat—"innuendo and rumor."

At Wang, IBM, and Digital, electronic mail only served to emphasize and strengthen the dysfunctional behaviors already taking place at these companies.

The problem isn't with the basic technology of electronic mail. The Electronic Elite know how to use electronic mail to strengthen their already powerful corporate cultures. They do this by using electronic mail to build flatter organizational structures and as a vehicle for dispersing power downward into the company. I asked former Microsoft executive vice president Mike Maples how the use of electronic mail there differed from the way it was used inside the traditional vendors such as Wang and IBM:

> When you commit a high percentage of your communication to electronic mail—as we do at Microsoft—then you process a lot more transactions per day. You don't have 15-minute meetings on one-minute subjects. You have better control of your time and are more likely to hear about things that you need to know about. Electronic mail encourages, but doesn't require, a much flatter, much more democratic kind of organization. To some extent, the acceptance of that organizational change is probably one of the most important elements. I don't think electronic mail makes you do that, but it allows you to do that. If you still have a strict hierarchical organization, and you're allowed to send mail only to your boss, and your boss forwards it to his boss, and you go through the organizational disciplines and protocols that were established in the old days, then it hasn't helped you.

The lesson is this: *Electronic mail doesn't solve problems—it accelerates communication.* If the communications behavior inside a company is fundamentally productive, then chances are, electronic mail will make it more productive. If, however, the communications inside a company are dysfunctional, then electronic mail may make things worse. Microsoft's Bill Gates put it best:

> I predict that, by 2005, the world will be your office—and your marketplace. In this new business environment, managers will no longer be able to use information as a means to control employees; in fact, this old-style manager is already becoming extinct as organizations flatten, and empowered employee workgroups become common in the many reengineered organizations of the 1990s.

The impact, then—positive or negative—of e-mail depends on the dominant mindsets within an organization. Companies that have internalized the traditional business culture will find that electronic mail strengthens those behaviors, detailed here:

1. *Business=Battlefield.* Companies use electronic mail to strengthen chains of command and to conduct internal political battles. Result: The company becomes inwardly focused and increasingly paranoid of "enemies."
2. *Corporation=Machine.* Companies use electronic mail to set up automated procedures that inhibit human initiative. Result: Employees become even more alienated and disconnected from the organization's goals.
3. *Management=Control.* Companies use electronic mail to micromanage projects, thus ensuring compliance with established rules and regulations. Result: The company becomes increasingly inflexible as power concentrates at the top.
4. *Employee=Child.* Companies use electronic mail to monitor daily activities of employees. Result: Employees resent the scrutiny and focus on "getting away with things."
5. *Motivation=Fear.* Companies use electronic mail to disseminate and augment fear-based rumors and displays of anger. Result: Employees become enmeshed in internal politics and self-preservation, to the neglect of customers.
6. *Change=Pain.* Companies use electronic mail to formalize and automate business processes that support the status quo, thereby

making change more difficult. Result: The organization becomes more difficult to change.

By contrast, the corporate culture of the Electronic Elite is perfectly suited to use electronic mail effectively:

1. *Business=Ecosystem.* Companies use electronic mail—and the Internet—to identify new opportunities and develop businesses to exploit them. Result: Consistent and profitable growth through the rapid development of new opportunities.
2. *Corporation=Community.* Companies use electronic mail to help people build healthy internal and external relationships. Result: Employees (even at remote sites) feel loyal and dedicated to the organization's goals.
3. *Management=Service.* Companies use electronic mail to make management more accessible. Result: Employees feel connected to and supported by management, not smothered by it.
4. *Employee=Peer.* Companies use electronic mail to disperse responsibility and authority to employee "businesses." Result: Employees claim ownership of their projects.
5. *Motivation=Vision.* Companies use electronic mail to share positive experiences and proliferate the vision. Result: Employees become more focused and dedicated.
6. *Change=Growth.* Companies use electronic mail to expand organizational boundaries of communication. Result: Communications flow more freely, enabling everyone to learn and adapt more quickly.

The Electronic Elite companies, in short, use electronic mail as a powerful vehicle for cultural adaptation and change, rather than to buttress the status quo. Former Lotus CEO Jim Manzi commented on this:

> The nature of modern office technology challenges the fundamental power associations in the organization, because information that used to be the source of people's power is now shareable— and it should be shared. The greatest challenge is to evoke the idea that information sharing is better than information hoarding.

Information sharing makes for better products, better customer service, better employee morale, and so forth. It is a fundamental challenge to basic hierarchical, command-and-control, power-oriented thinking that has characterized organizations for 2,000 years.

The Electronic Elite rely on four primary strategies to use the new office technology effectively. The first provides the grand vision of how the Electronic Elite use electronic mail. The other three strategies provide valuable advice for using electronic mail effectively, within the context of an elite culture.

- Create an electronic community.
- Handle e-mail with care.
- Keep it short and simple.
- Ruthlessly prioritize.

STRATEGY 28: CREATE AN ELECTRONIC COMMUNITY

To the Electronic Elite, electronic mail is much more than a faster way to send memos. It is a way of implementing the kind of responsive and flexible organizations that are most likely to react productively to market conditions. Software venture capitalist and industry savant Ann Winblad told me:

> At Microsoft, communication pervades the entire organization. There's no Microsoft executive or employee who doesn't travel with a notebook computer, and they're constantly checking their electronic mail. Electronic mail routes around that company at all levels. Electronic mail allows the organization to be much flatter from a communications standpoint than in the traditional company.

Former Microsoft executive vice president Mike Maples commented that electronic mail has been a vehicle for keeping Microsoft free of the kind of political infighting that freezes many Industrial Age companies:

> The electronic mail system has the consequences of eliminating organizational politics, which flourish when you tell one person

one thing and another person something else. When you have a flat organization where everybody's in the discussion all the time, the number of "side deals" are greatly minimized. Because what somebody says is so easily copied and redistributed, people have to be much clearer and much more direct, merely because the mechanism for distribution of the information is so efficient. We try not to have competing missions or competing objectives. We try not to have one organization viewing another organization as their competition or in the way of their success. You can never have that perfect, but we work real hard at trying to "empower" the teams to do their own thing.

The same can be true in a smaller company. For example, CEO Sally Narodick explained how Edmark uses electronic mail to keep people involved in the decision-making process:

We make tremendous use of voice mail and e-mail, and we've invested a fair amount of time to get it up and running. It has paid for itself a thousandfold in terms of helping teams work together. There are so many things that you can do with the new technology: You can make sure everybody's briefed, or has a chance to present his or her angle of the topic into the discussion. We believe that information is power and try to make key business information available broadly. We have our own homegrown groupware that we use to share documents and files. It's the heart of what we do in our culture and how we manage. Thanks to these vehicles, almost no one goes through a hierarchical structure to talk to another person or to review things. We just chatter across all different kinds of lines to get things done, to brief people, to get input.

Another heavy user of electronic mail is Sun Microsystems. CEO Scott McNealy is so "plugged in" to his electronic mail system that he doesn't even put it aside when he's being interviewed. Here's what Scott told me when I asked him about electronic mail usage at Sun:

We have an e-mail culture, so information is distributed immediately and massively throughout the company. For example, while you and I were talking, I just got an e-mail that told me what the stock price was today when the market closed. I had another flash this morning about IBM pulling the Pentium chip off the market. You have so much instantaneous access. I don't have to wait for the newspaper to come out. All the stuff that I need to know just starts showing up on my e-mail. E-mail also allows us to run a flatter organization because we can get everybody rolling in the same cadence, because the information out there is so much more clear.

The Electronic Elite aren't afraid to put the power of electronic mail into the hands of all their employees. Mike Maples commented:

At Microsoft, anybody that needs to be aware of a subject anywhere in the organization is copied on the original piece of mail. This tends to short-circuit the filtering of information. You have a much faster movement of information from the time of an action to the time that everybody knows about the action. It encourages people at multiple levels to enter the debate simultaneously so you don't have to have a workgroup debate an issue, take it to the manager, debate the issue again, take it to another manager, for more debate, and filter it up the chain of command. Instead, decision making happens in real time with people at all levels in the organization.

Ideally, electronic mail becomes a vehicle for the rapid decision making that's so important to an Electronic Elite organization. However, if electronic mail is to be used in this way, the people using the system must be able to use it effectively. And that's the subject of the next three strategies.

STRATEGY 29: HANDLE E-MAIL WITH CARE

Electronic mail can be a powerful tool. However, like all power tools, it must be used with caution. The constant ebb and flow of electronic mail communication presents wonderful opportunities, but also significant dangers.

The ability to communicate with anyone in the organization gives you a level and speed of visibility that means, in a matter of seconds, you can either make a complete fool of yourself in front of everybody on the network, or be regarded with respect and admiration for your ideas and ability to express them.

In particular, managers must be careful using electronic mail, which if not handled appropriately can make them less effective. William Campbell, CEO of Intuit, told me:

> I worked with an executive who managed by e-mail. He'd read a report or something in his e-mail folder, disagree with it, and then send a memo to the effect that "I think this is the stupidest thing I've ever read." And he'd blast it out to six people in the group. As a result, each person in the group would write him another two-to-three page e-mail message attempting to explain why the report was valid. Everybody would spend 45 minutes thoughtfully banging out an electronic answer. And, invariably, he would find out that the original memo was on target and that the group had thought the situation through very carefully. I don't know how many hours we wasted answering electronic messages just to address something that could have been settled during a brief hallway conversation.

It's especially important to remember to control your temper when you use electronic mail. Never write a piece of electronic mail when you're hot under the collar. Go for a walk. Take a shower. Play solitaire. Do anything except write electronic mail. You'll thank yourself in the morning. One touch of the send button, and your "flame-o-gram" has been written into the pages of corporate history. And you just might be history yourself, because there's no way you're ever going to get that message back. Until somebody invents a "heat-seeking e-mail missile," the most you can do is write an apology, which, if you're lucky, will convince people that you were suffering from a momentary lapse of judgment.

Another indiscretion that electronic mail can foster is what's come to be called a "mail war." Mail wars occur when two or more employees argue electronically, and make the argument public by sending copies of all the messages and responses to various managers and co-workers whom the combatants wish to enlist in the controversy. This kind of behavior can be extremely debilitating and must be dealt with quickly, according to Jonathan Seybold, former president of Seybold Seminars:

> My organization depends on lateral communication and teamwork. E-mail is really very important to facilitate that. On the whole, it works very well for us. When there are problems, we have to take care of them. We had two people who were not getting along, not cooperating. Our e-mail system became a way of lobbing hand grenades over the wall. E-mail is a far more destructive means of communication when the communication is negative, first, because it is less personal and more easily misconstrued; and second, because it brings other people into the fray. We talked with the two individuals—in person, not via e-mail—and told them that their behavior was not acceptable. We counseled them, but, eventually, because of what the e-mail wars were reflecting, both of them had to leave the company.

STRATEGY 30: KEEP IT SHORT AND SIMPLE

Even when an organization is careful with its use of electronic mail, it can become an unnecessary burden to employees. Remember, electronic mail is only part of a revolution in office technology, which has resulted in an extraordinary explosion of information. According to Boston-based Delphi Consulting Group, which specializes in document management and workflow, computers now produce over one *billion* pages of output a day in the United States alone. To put this into perspective, a billion pages laid end-to-end would circle the earth 20 times. Stacked in reams, it would tower 10 times higher than Mount Everest. The worldwide amount of paper output in just two seconds would fill the average office, ceiling to floor.

This quantity of information makes it difficult to find the right material at the right time. According to Robert Half Consulting, senior executives now spend over an hour each day searching for information. Some professionals, according to time management guru Alec Mackenzie, spend approximately 94 days a year just handling paperwork.

PLUGGERS by Jeff MacNelly

The information revolution is over.
Information won.

Reprinted by permission: Tribune Media Services.

Electronic mail can, to a degree, replace paper memoranda with electronic versions, but there are some features and characteristics of electronic mail that, if not held in check, can make the problem of information overload even worse. Keep in mind that with a single keystroke, e-mail users can send a message to a distribution list containing hundreds of recipients. When the information justifies that kind of distribution, it's great, but often employees overestimate the importance of what they have to communicate. This results in electronic junk mail that, just like its paper predecessor, clutters up the system, making it difficult and unpleasant to find the really important materials.

The solution is to encourage employees to use the electronic mail system responsibly, which may require setting some guidelines for proper usage. This isn't to say that management should dictate a set of rules; the challenge is to make the electronic mail system more effective. Therefore, employees should be consulted to define a workable set of guidelines. The following may help as a start:

1. *Inform, don't overload.* Constantly ask yourself: "Do these people really need to know this bit of information?" Don't gain a reputation as someone who sends out lots of meaningless messages. People will start deleting your messages, unread, assuming they're not important. Far better to be the kind of person who sends electronic mail only when it's really relevant. That way your messages will get read first.

2. *Use a descriptive mail header.* A mail header is the title of the message that appears in the recipient's list of new mail. Create a header that explains briefly and clearly what the message is about. Recipients are often so swamped with mail messages that they rely on the headers to sort through them.

3. *Keep messages short and well-thought-out.* If possible, write a message that's no longer than the size of the average screen display. If you must communicate something lengthier, summarize the document in the first screen and end that first screen with "details to follow." Electronic mail messages should be written like newspaper stories: headlines first, followed by the main points, followed by the details in decreasing order of importance.

Make these guidelines a part of your business culture and you'll be well on the way to staying afloat on the sea of information. Those interested in additional guidelines for writing effective electronic mail communications should consider the book *The Elements of E-mail Style,* by David Angell and Brent Heslop.

STRATEGY 31: RUTHLESSLY PRIORITIZE

Avoiding mail wars and keeping communications to a manageable minimum won't eliminate the problem of information overload completely, but they can make the problem less overwhelming. As the recipient of electronic mail, you'll also have to find a way to manage your mailbox. You may find it useful to constantly prioritize the information that you receive. One way to do this is to refuse to spend time reading mail messages that aren't pertinent to the tasks at hand. This is particularly useful if you know how to speed-read, according to Scott McNealy, CEO of Sun Microsystems:

> I've never known anybody to fail because they had too much information to make a decision. I think e-mail is great, but because I can speed-read, any topic I'm not interested in, I click, and it's gone. If it's something I need to know, I read it immediately. If it's something I can deal with later, I either print it out or load it into a laptop and take it with me. I've never had too much information.

Prioritizing is much easier, of course, if you work for a company that has a clear vision and a clear mission. If these two things are vague, prioritization is difficult, because you can't know what's likely to be important. That's another reason that the Electronic Elite organize employees into autonomous teams. Team goals preclude an entire staff from having to be involved in the day-to-day communications of each group, thus making it easier for people to prioritize information.

Even if your organization isn't as focused as it could be, it's up to you individually to develop the self-discipline to prioritize your time so that you don't become involved in electronic discussions that, while interesting, aren't immediately important. Former Microsoft executive VP Mike Maples commented:

> You must decide that there are some debates that, while you might be able to contribute and while they are important, you just don't have the time to become involved in. You become an observer or you ignore them.

It's also a good idea to prioritize before the fact. If you're getting too many mail messages every day, it may be because you're on too many distribution lists. Well-meaning folks are sending you information that you really don't need to know. Ask to be taken off any distribution lists that you don't need to be on. If you're a manager, specify which types of messages or content you must see, and remove yourself from phases of communication that don't require your input. This action has the added benefit of showing that you trust people to do their jobs.

The key to not becoming overwhelmed by the flow of information is to be personally organized. Software venture capitalist Ann Winblad commented:

> Personal organization is key to survival. I have voice mail. I have electronic mail. I have Federal Express. I have the mailman. And, by the end of the day, my desk is crowded. If I did not have good personal organization skills, I'd be toast. It is a requirement in flat, free-flowing, participatory organizations. People who have great personal organization skills and can manage the overload are the people who stand out.

This chapter explained how to turn electronic mail from a possible productivity burden into a positive productivity accelerator. This builds a framework for the final phase—that of achieving a balance between work and personal life.

Chapter Eleven

Create a Sense
of Balance

The Electronic Elite have an extremely optimistic view of the office of the future. The practice what they preach—and sell—and thus feel confident that electronic mail, voice mail, cellular phones, and portable computers will make organizations more productive. They're predicting that the office technology of the future is destined to change the business world. Here's how Microsoft Chairman Bill Gates put it:

> In the office of the future, intelligent applications, high-bandwidth networks, and innovative devices will connect people and information wherever they are—homes, cars, or public kiosks. For example, a "virtual team" of experts around the world could work together to produce a report. They could meet, pass information, documents, images, and large files back and forth—or review them together—saving the time and expense of travel. The network becomes their "virtual conference room." Smaller central offices, more cost-effective ways to train and communicate with employees, and greater flexibility in reaching customers, add up to a better bottom line for business. Businesses will also have greater access to global resources. This means getting precisely the right information and people for every job—and increasing productivity and quality.

Bill is talking about mobile computing, using computer technology to free people to work almost anywhere, either as individual contributors or in teams. For example, I wrote a good part of this book sitting on a hillside deck overlooking the woods of New Hampshire and on the cliffs overlooking the ocean in Los Angeles. Being able to work and write in different places gives me greater flexibility to live my life the way I want to live it. Because I'm not tied to a physical location, I can use my time more effectively. I can't remember the last time I boarded an airplane without a notebook computer and some work to keep me busy on the trip.

The downside of this, however, is that it sometimes becomes difficult to maintain boundaries between work and personal time. All too frequently, people take work with them everywhere or are never out of reach of the office because of ubiquitous mobile communications equipment.

According to Harvard economist Juliet Schor, employees in the United States now work an average 164 hours longer a year now than they did in 1970, before computers came on the scene. This reflects a disturbing trend of many businesses, which are becoming intolerant of vacation and off-hours. Mobile computing pressures professionals in many industries to literally work around the clock. Who hasn't seen and pitied the bleary-eyed walking wounded, lugging their portable computers through airport lobbies in the wee hours of the morning?

This is troubling, because significant health problems are connected with highly automated work environments. According to an August 1992 article in *Supervision* magazine, a study of 11 women in an automated office revealed that they had a rate of miscarriage that was astronomically higher than the rest of the population. An article in *Office Systems* magazine (August 1991) warned that the rise in office automation in today's business has been matched by a rise in computer-related health complaints: headaches, muscle fatigue, blurred vision, repetitive stress injuries, carpal tunnel syndrome, tendinitis, and lower back pain.

The combination of long work hours and computer-related health problems can create an unhealthy work environment. Electronic Elite employees haven't been immune from these problems. On the contrary, the Electronic Elite know that there is an ever-present danger of burnout inside their organizations. While they believe that long work hours remain necessary, they also know that they must avoid burnout and ill health. Thus, the Electronic Elite try to encourage a sense of balance inside their organizations. Mitchell Kertzman, CEO of Powersoft, commented:

> My philosophy is that you've got to have balance between your work life and your personal life. I want people to work very hard when they're here, and they do. But I want them to be as happy at home as at work, and to be as giving to their families as they are to Powersoft. In the long run, that creates the best work environment. Happy people do the best work. Balanced people do the best work. So, it's very important to me that people have that balance.

As the Electronic Elite workforce ages, the attractiveness of the late-night-with-coffee-and-pizza work sessions begins to wear thin. This is not to say that they're not working as hard as they used to do. It's only that they've come to a better understanding of the need for a sense of balance in their lives. The following case study illustrates the consequence of not maintaining a balanced existence.

CASE STUDY: APPLE COMPUTER AND THE MACINTOSH GRAPHICAL USER INTERFACE

In the early 1980s, one of the exciting start-ups was Apple Computer. Founded by two young men in a California garage, Apple grew to be one of the most famous success stories of the computer industry. Cofounder and former president Steven Jobs believed that computing could become far simpler than it was at the time and he envisioned people being able to interact with computers as easily as they do with other common household appliances.

Job's vision became the Macintosh personal computer, a device that changed the way that we use computers. Although other fancy computers had preceded it, the Macintosh was the first inexpensive and practical computer to use a graphical user interface (GUI). The Macintosh GUI introduced the concept of icons. If you wanted to access a program, you pointed at an icon using a handheld mouse and clicked a button. This point-and-click interface, while common today, was virtually unknown outside research laboratories at that time.

When the Macintosh was launched, the most common personal computer was the IBM PC—as it is today. The IBM PC ran an operating system called MS-DOS, a Microsoft product that required users to access programs by typing cryptic commands. Because the Macintosh was so much easier to use, Apple was able to charge a premium price for it, which made Apple among the most profitable companies in the computer industry.

However, Apple's ability to charge a premium price for the Macintosh was dependent on the clumsiness of MS-DOS. As soon as Microsoft's Windows version 3.0 hit the market in 1990, fewer users were willing to pay more for a Macintosh. Microsoft Windows, while not as easy to use as the Macintosh GUI, was still good enough to erode Apple's competitive advantage. Apple was forced to drop prices. Profit margins began to suffer and Apple's stock took a serious dip.

Apple could have stolen Microsoft's thunder if it had had the foresight to recode the Macintosh GUI so that it could run on the Intel-based IBM PC. This would have diminished the impact of Windows and likely would have propelled Apple into the highly favorable position that Microsoft enjoys today. True, in porting the Macintosh GUI, Apple would still have had to drop the price of the Macintosh hardware, but this would have become necessary in any case. Far better for Apple to lead the way than to be forced to react to Microsoft.

Why didn't Apple make this all-important move? To understand this, you need to understand Apple's corporate culture. Apple founder Steven Jobs was a management visionary. As the head of the Macintosh project, Steve installed in his employees an overwhelming desire to make the product successful. Long work hours were the norm. In 1983, the Macintosh development team wore T-shirts emblazoned with the motto: "Working 90 hours a week and loving every minute of it."

This enthusiasm had a downside as well. The long hours—once a matter of pride—had become an expectation; Apple became an unhealthy place in which to work. One rumor had it that certain managers had begun measuring productivity by the number of divorces in their group—the more divorces, the harder their people were working. Statistics bear this out: The divorce rate in Silicon Valley, where Apple was located, was "unsurpassed" according to Dennis Hayes, writing in the book *Behind the Silicon Curtain: The Seductions of Work in a Lonely Era.* This kind of insensitivity to normal human needs had predictable consequences. By 1988, according to Hayes, an estimated 65 percent of Apple employees were "in therapy." The situation had gotten so bad that Apple was soliciting bids for an on-site psychotherapy facility.

The long hours and relentless self-sacrificing zealotry had turned many key Apple employees into exhausted, burned-out veterans. Under these circumstances, it's almost inevitable that Apple would stumble sooner or later. And stumble it did, at the worst time possible, just when the first real competition to its famous interface was about to be born.

Although many other factors contributed to Apple's ill-fated decision, the burnout of many Apple employees undoubtedly was a key problem. Employees who are burned out and unhealthy are likely to make poor decisions. Creativity dries up. The free flow of ideas— which is critical for success—becomes blocked. People running on automatic become irrational. Relationships break down inside the worker's family, between co-workers, customers, and suppliers. This is why the Electronic Elite encourage a sense of balance, both in their own lives, and in the lives of their employees. In my conversations with the Electronic Elite, we discussed the specific strategies that they use:

• Cultivate constant challenge.
• Learn to disconnect.
• Take frequent sabbaticals.

Strategy 32: Cultivate Constant Challenge

The Electronic Elite believe that the source of the employee's motivation makes a big difference in whether or not long work hours lead to burnout. Employees who work hard because they *want* to work hard are much less likely to burn out than employees who work hard because they *have* to work hard. Thus the Electronic Elite try to set up work situations where long hours aren't perceived as a burden because the work is interesting and challenging. Scott McNealy, CEO of Sun Microsystems, put it this way:

> The only way you get burned out is when you have a frustrating or boring job. I know human nature well enough to know that if you give people 50 decks of cards all shuffled together and say, I want you to shuffle them, then sort them out into the proper decks in proper order, then reshuffle them, and do that again all day long, then you will have somebody burned out within four hours. But if you put them in a challenging job where they're learning along the way, driving new technologies and solving interesting customer problems, they'll go home with a big smile on their faces, feeling great about themselves, feeling great about what they've done, feeling great about what they've learned. If you have a fair, honest, diverse, equitable, challenging, exciting work environment, there's nothing more you can do to pump someone up. They just walk with a bounce in their step. I've never felt bad about working somebody hard when we're working on fun stuff.

Sally Narodick, CEO of Edmark, agreed:

> We try to help people keep going until the product ships. It's a very goal-driven organization but we try to be people-sensitive and value people and their families. But the truth is that to work in this business you need to be someone who has a passion about making this happen and who wants to contribute entrepreneurial drive to be able to survive here. We try to do it in a way that lets people give a lot of what they have to give and really be valued. If you're using a good portion of your human potential and if you're valued for your ideas, work is energizing, not draining. That's what we try to do.

In my many years of working with the companies of the Electronic Elite, I've met an amazing number of employees who were energized and jazzed by their jobs, more than in any other industry. When I compare the attitude of an average Microsoft or Powersoft or Novell or COMPAQ employee with that of the average worker on the street, I can't help but believe that the Electronic Elite are onto a powerful force leading toward a healthier and more productive workplace.

This is not to say that every Electronic Elite employee is in love with his or her job. People work long hours for different reasons. Some employees work long hours because they have a financial stake in the corporation. If the company does well, then they'll be rewarded richly. Other employees work long hours because they want to impress their peers. And some employees, even in Electronic Elite organizations, work long hours merely because it's expected of them. The Electronic Elite, however, try to make every job interesting and challenging.

STRATEGY 33: LEARN TO DISCONNECT

Even if you're enjoying work, it's important to maintain a sense of balance. Michael Dell, CEO of Dell Computer, explained:

> This is a very challenging business that continues to present me and everyone that's involved in it with opportunities to learn and grow. We're always doing something that's very exciting and new, whether it's expanding in Asia or launching into a new product segment. However, there's a limit to the number of productive hours a person can actually work. There's also only so much fun you can have before it starts to be not as much fun.

Because long working hours are sometimes going to be the rule, the Electronic Elite make it a habit to disconnect from work on a regular basis. Some simply won't take work home with them. They leave their home life as a haven away from work, turning the abbreviated time with their families into "quality" time. Jim Manzi, former CEO of Lotus, commented on how he does this in his own life.

I come to work very early in the morning, and, if I'm not traveling, I go home for dinner, and I don't bring work home. It's as simple as that. I can't work any harder than I do, and if I tried, I would just be pretending. I spend an enormous amount of time and energy on this place but there are limits. I communicate it openly in the company that everybody has to find their own balance. It's an individual decision about how you want to be in your own life and how you want to balance yourself. It's not some law that I will dictate. I believe in individuals making their own decisions about what's important in their lives and finding their own point of balance and making those trade-offs.

Ann Palermo, vice president of worldwide marketing for the PC-DOCS document management software company (and a mother of two), takes a similar approach:

I don't talk about work at all when I'm at home. I've learned to pick up at 5:30 and leave the office. You have to be able to accept that work will never be finished. Nothing is ever "done." Some people think of it as a treadmill, but I know that even if I spend three times as much time at the office, there would still be more to do. You can't be home on the weekend thinking "I'll never get this project done." You just have to be able to leave it alone. It's a mental discipline, I suppose, although some people might say that I'm in denial. I don't know how people survive without being able to set it aside.

For the Electronic Elite who practice this strategy, keeping their home life sacred helps creates a sense of balance and perspective. By setting aside their work for a while, they find it easier to be productive when they return to their demanding schedules.

Electronic Elite employees often have hobbies and interests that help them forget work for a while. Former Microsoft executive vice president Mike Maples described how he sees the employees at Microsoft:

One of the things that's really hard to represent about Microsoft is the dimensions of the characters and the interests that the people have. Most books make its characters pretty unidimensional. But, like any place, the people at Microsoft have a lot of dimensions.

There are a lot of musicians around, people with weird hobbies, virtually anything you can think of. The trade-off that people make at a Microsoft is that they have three or four passions rather than a dozen passions that are important to them in life. Whether those passions are family, or church, or activities, or hobbies, or mountain climbing or whatever, almost everybody at Microsoft has a number of things that interest them beside Microsoft. However, the number of those things is probably less than at other companies.

The key is make certain that you have some way to temporarily disconnect from the demanding ebb and flow of work. Industry guru Jonathan Seybold explained how he achieves this balance:

> You've got to moderate yourself. There are times when I very deliberately do not read my electronic mail or answer my voice mail. There are other times when we have something important taking place, where I will check in during the weekend several times. When there's breaking news, you want to tune in and find out what's happening. In the same way, if there's a decision to make, we can get a lot done between Friday night and Monday morning. However, you only want to do that when there's something going on that makes it worthwhile. If you get in a habit of doing it all the time, you'll never have good decisions. You end up spending more of your time cleaning up messes and having less of your resources available to really get things done.

STRATEGY 34: TAKE FREQUENT SABBATICALS

Work at Electronic Elite companies often has seasonal rhythms based on whether a new product is under development, or there is a spate of trade shows to attend, and so forth. One way to achieve balance, according to the Electronic Elite, is to match the rhythms of life to the rhythms of work. Carol Bartz, CEO of AutoDesk, commented on this challenge:

> People spend too much of their time trying to be the perfect executive, or the perfect technologist, the perfect mom or dad, the perfect partner, the perfect corporate citizen or social citizen, and so

forth. If you try to pull off all that stuff every day or every week, you will burn out. There's no doubt about it. There are times, for example, when you've got a product to release, when you've got to say to your family, "I'll see you in a month." There are other times when you've got to say to the company, "I've got a new baby, or my daughter's having her birthday party and I'll see you next week." You have to figure out how to change your priorities and not make everything be as important as everything else all the time. It doesn't mean that home is more important than work or work more important than home. It just means that you have to take each of them singularly.

Electronic Elite leaders promote a better sense of balance is by giving employees a certain amount of flexibility about coming into work, especially when things are slow. Bill Gross, CEO of Knowledge Adventure explained:

I'm definitely concerned about people becoming burned out. We have been able to manage that by still giving people complementary time off when they finish a crunch project. We also try to stagger the cycles of the crunches so that people can rejuvenate. When people are simply too exhausted to do their work here, mobile computing allows them to work from Lake Tahoe or from home for a few days to recuperate but still stay in touch without delaying a project.

Some companies even sanction sabbaticals that give employees the opportunity to collect their thoughts and reestablish balance in their lives. Carol Bartz, CEO of AutoDesk, told about the program in her company:

After four years, people get a 6-week sabbatical, which they often combine with their vacation to take 8 or 10 weeks off. That can be very controversial, and I've heard other companies say that people don't come back and so forth. However, I think that a sabbatical really does revive people. It gives them a chance to get away for a couple of months, get a perspective on things, travel around the world, spend time with their families, live with a newborn, whatever, and people tend to come back really energized. I make a strong statement in a lot of my speeches about balance.

Silicon Graphics also has an official sabbatical program. CEO Edward McCracken believes that this is one reason that the company has such a loyal group of employees:

> Our employee turnover is extremely low. It's a high morale environment. We have a sabbatical program, where every four years everybody gets to take six weeks off with pay to do something they haven't done. We try to give people a break so that we don't have too much burnout, even though people work very hard here.

This chapter has described how to evolve a corporate culture that is not only flexible and productive, but healthy and humane for its staff as well. The computerization of the business world has created new challenges for employees, who must cope with new technology as well as with additional demands on their time. Encouraging a sense of balance helps ensure that productivity will be sustained over time and helps ensure that employees will remain motivated and energized, ready to take on the challenges of fast-moving markets.

Epilogue

By the end of our lives, we will have spent approximately a quarter of our waking hours at work, more time than we're likely to spend doing anything else. Do we really want to spend this precious time working at jobs we don't enjoy, with peers we don't trust, for bosses we secretly despise?

Wherever I go, I meet people who are deeply dissatisfied with their jobs, who feel underutilized yet overworked, patronized and pandered to, apathetic and unmotivated. I see middle managers who are lonely, unhappy, and paranoid, who hate their jobs yet are terrified of losing them. I watch executives who, despite their high salaries, are dazed and confused, following business strategies that have long since lost their meaning and effectiveness. How sad and yet how unnecessary!

A corporate culture is reestablished every day when people go to work under the same mindsets. Most don't realize—or believe—they are free to choose new ways of doing business that will lead toward greater success in the future. So why don't more companies make the transition to a more powerful and flexible culture? Why do they wait until the market forces change upon them?

Traditional business culture often results in a Catch-22 situation in which the mindsets must change before the mindsets can change. People who have internalized the old culture have deep-seated beliefs that change is dangerous, complicated, and painful. They can't believe that everything could change *immediately*, if the people within the culture simply decided to adopt, and act on, a new set of beliefs.

In fact, it *is* that simple. The process of cultural transformation is nothing more than a series of personal decisions, made by people throughout an organization, to think about problems in new ways. If even one person has the courage to laugh out loud at a pompous presentation, or the wisdom to treat fellow workers as respected peers, an organization becomes more healthy. The challenge is one of leadership, not just at the top of the organization, but everywhere people interact and work together. It requires that people make a choice, a *decision* about what they really want.

That decision may require leaving your current position and finding employment in an organization that's better adapted to the Information Age and your way of thinking. But if you remain where you are, it's your responsibility and obligation to use the knowledge you've obtained and whatever leadership ability you possess to help create a workplace that's productive, humane, and fun.

A phrase that you hear a lot at Electronic Elite companies is "we're going to change the world." The Electronic Elite and their employees know that computer technology is making an incredible impact on every aspect of our daily lives. The Electronic Elite see the pace of innovation moving faster every year as raw computer power becomes ever less expensive. However, the Electronic Elite also know that it's the culture, not the technology, that determines how effectively that technology is used.

Technology is an enabler rather than a driver of cultural change: It's regrettable that so much attention is given to the products of the Electronic Elite and so little to the unique cultures that they've created. This book, I hope, begins to remedy this oversight. A hundred years from now, Bill Gates and all his colleagues will be history, and today's computers will be gathering dust in museums. In the long run, the legacy of the Electronic Elite may not be their technology, but this new corporate culture. Perhaps that's what the Electronic Elite *really* mean when they say "we're going to change the world."

Be part of the transformation!

Appendixes

Appendixes

Appendix I

The Mindset Shifts That Lead to Success

SHIFT 1: BUSINESS IS AN ECOSYSTEM, NOT A BATTLEFIELD

TRADITIONAL:
BUSINESS=BATTLEFIELD

Business is a series of conflicts among companies competing in a market, among departments in a company, among groups in an organization, among individuals in a group and—by extension—among customers and vendors.

ELECTRONIC ELITE:
BUSINESS=ECOSYSTEM

The business world is made up of symbiotic relationships formed to exploit market niches. The company that is the most diverse and partners best is the most likely to survive and thrive.

SHIFT 2: THE CORPORATION IS A COMMUNITY, NOT A MACHINE

TRADITIONAL:
CORPORATION=MACHINE

A corporation is a system in which employees are faceless cogs. Nobody is indispensable; everybody is replaceable. Individual initiative, goals, and desires are completely subsumed by the demands of the corporate machine.

ELECTRONIC ELITE:
CORPORATION=COMMUNITY

A company is a collection of individuals with individual hopes and dreams that are connected to their organization's higher purpose.

SHIFT 3: MANAGEMENT IS SERVICE, NOT CONTROL

TRADITIONAL:
MANAGEMENT=CONTROL

The real job of the manager is to control employee behavior. Employees who disagree with a manager or refuse to do something are "insubordinate" and dangerous.

ELECTRONIC ELITE:
MANAGEMENT=SERVICE

A manager's job is to set a direction and to obtain the resources that employees need to get the job done. Management wants to *lead* rather than *run* the organization. Dissent is encouraged so long as it resolves itself with creative ideas.

SHIFT 4: EMPLOYEES ARE PEERS, NOT CHILDREN

TRADITIONAL:
EMPLOYEE=CHILD

Employees cannot be trusted with real authority. Furthermore, they can't be trusted on any level. If not constrained by a complicated set of rules and regulations, they'll steal the company blind.

ELECTRONIC ELITE:
EMPLOYEE=PEER

Every employee is hired—regardless of position—as if he or she were the most important person in the company. Excellence is expected and encouraged everywhere, from the loading dock to the boardroom.

SHIFT 5: MOTIVATE WITH VISION, NOT FEAR

TRADITIONAL:
MOTIVATION=FEAR

Employees work only because they're afraid. Managers must therefore use fear—fear of getting fired, fear of ridicule, fear of loss of privilege—to motivate them.

ELECTRONIC ELITE:
MOTIVATION=VISION

People know where they're going, so the process of working is filled with energy, enthusiasm, and humor.

SHIFT 6: CHANGE IS GROWTH, NOT PAIN

TRADITIONAL:
CHANGE=PAIN

ELECTRONIC ELITE:
CHANGE=GROWTH

Change is seen as complicated and difficult, and is considered something that should be implemented as a last resort.

Change is a wonderful thing because it's part of the process of adapting to new market conditions and growing into new levels of success.

Appendix II

The Stages of Building an Elite Corporate Culture

STAGE 1: REDEFINE YOUR CURRENT CULTURE

In this stage, you decide what kind of culture your organization needs to have to achieve its goals. This requires examining your current culture, finding role models for your new culture, brainstorming to create a new cultural definition, and soliciting the participation of the rest of the organization in the cultural definition process.

STAGE 2: BREAK LIMITING CULTURAL PATTERNS

In this stage, you eliminate the roadblocks that prevent your organization from adopting the ideal culture that you've helped it envision. To accomplish this, you confront and overcome pockets of denial, take dramatic actions that emphasize that the organization has a new culture, build a new vocabulary that fits the new culture and, most important, implement processes and procedures that are congruent with the new culture.

Stage 3: Harness Electronic Mail

In this stage, you either install, or revisit, your electronic communications capability and make certain that it's used in a way that strengthens your new culture. This means using the electronic mail system to build a stronger sense of community, making certain that people use electronic mail productively, and ensuring that the increase of information helps rather than hinders success.

Stage 4: Create a Sense of Balance

In this stage, you ensure that your culture doesn't create burnout among your self-motivated and productive employees. This means setting up formal and informal mechanisms to make certain that people can relax when overwhelmed. Most important, it means making certain that people are doing jobs that they truly enjoy.

Management Strategies of the Electronic Elite

STRATEGY 1: ENCOURAGE DIVERSITY

Create organizations where there is a diversity of opinion, background, and approach to solving problems. The more diverse an organization, the better it can adapt to changing market circumstances.

STRATEGY 2: LAUNCH NEW GENERATIONS

Don't cling to products and services that are successful today. Always be on the lookout for new products and services that will make your current winners obsolete. Then become the company that develops those new products and services.

STRATEGY 3: BUILD SYMBIOTIC RELATIONSHIPS

Craft business arrangements so that everybody benefits. When business is treated as a zero-sum game, with a winner and loser, even the so-called winner eventually loses. When business is treated as a symbiosis, then markets and profits grow all around you.

STRATEGY 4: COMMUNICATE DIRECTLY

Promote regular contact between executives and line employees, so that all members of the organization—even the people working on the loading dock—feel deeply connected to the goals and direction of the corporation.

STRATEGY 5: CREATE OPPORTUNITIES FOR SOCIAL INTERACTION

Encourage employees to set up social functions where there's a lot of intergroup mingling. It's especially important that top management get involved in this, so that they become an important part of the connected social network.

STRATEGY 6: MAKE WORK FUN

Lighten up and make work into a good time. People naturally like to spend time where they're having fun. If work is something that brings them pleasure then the corporation can't help but see higher productivity, less absenteeism, and a more positive social impact.

STRATEGY 7: INCREASE POWER BY DISPERSING IT

The more that management pushes power and decision-making authority "down" into the organizations, the more power and flexibility the entire corporation has.

STRATEGY 8: ENCOURAGE CREATIVE DISSENT

The combination of diversity of opinion and dispersion of power naturally creates an atmosphere where people disagree on the approaches to be taken. Make this dissent, and the resolution that inevitably follows, part of the process of creating new value.

STRATEGY 9: BUILD AUTONOMOUS TEAMS

Rather than organizing along broad functional lines, make certain that each product and service has a team that's dedicated to the success of that product and service. Make certain that the team actually has the decision-making power to get things done.

STRATEGY 10: HIRE THE SELF-MOTIVATED

When hiring and promoting, locate or cultivate people who don't require direction and who aren't spoiled by Industrial Age habits. This will help influence everybody else in the organization to act in a more independent fashion.

STRATEGY 11: ELIMINATE FANCY PERKS

Avoid the kind of perks that create distance between managers and employees. Integrate the management and executive staff into the base of employees so that everyone feels as if they are part of the same community.

STRATEGY 12: ENCOURAGE INFORMALITY

Put everybody on a first-name basis and let every day be "casual day." Create an environment where people feel as if they're at home with their friends and family. After all, isn't that what makes up a community?

STRATEGY 13: CREATE A CLIMATE OF TRUST

Look for opportunities to build trust between individuals, teams, and organizations. Always act in a way that's congruent with the positive ideal of the corporate culture.

STRATEGY 14: CREATE A SENSE OF MISSION

Make certain that there is a shared vision that resonates with everybody in the organization. Make sure that, within the context of that vision, everybody knows what mission they're supposed to be accomplishing.

STRATEGY 15: COMPENSATE FOR MISSIONS ACCOMPLISHED

Tie extra, team-based compensation to the accomplishment of the mission at hand, within the larger context of the corporate vision. Make certain that the success of the organization translates into the success of the individuals it includes.

STRATEGY 16: HAVE LONG-TERM VISION, SHORT-TERM PLANS

Look ahead to the future for guidance, but don't waste time mapping out a detailed plan to get there. Instead, concentrate on what needs to be done next to move you closer to your ultimate goal.

STRATEGY 17: KEEP JOBS FLUID AND FLEXIBLE

Don't bother writing detailed job descriptions and trying to set up a "system." Instead, let individuals, teams, and organizations define themselves as necessary to accomplish the job at hand.

STRATEGY 18: MAKE DECISIONS QUICKLY AND BROADLY

Promote an environment where important decisions receive lively debate from all levels of the organization. Then drive the decision to a close.

STRATEGY 19: HOPE FOR THE BEST, PREPARE FOR THE WORST

Make certain that everyone knows that layoffs are a fact of life. Encourage individuals and organizations to have contingency plans in case worse comes to worst.

STRATEGY 20: CALIBRATE YOUR CURRENT CULTURE

Constantly examine your current culture to see whether it matches the goals that your organization has set out to achieve.

STRATEGY 21: CULTIVATE CULTURAL ROLE MODELS

Examine the best companies both inside and outside your industry so that you can emulate the cultural attributes that will make your organization successful.

STRATEGY 22: IMAGINE THE POSSIBILITIES

Dare to aspire to a corporate culture that creates and encourages a productive, humane, flexible, and fun workplace.

STRATEGY 23: EXTEND THE VISION

Use the excitement, dedication and desires of everybody in the organization to transform the vision of a new culture into an everyday reality.

STRATEGY 24: DIRECTLY CONFRONT DENIAL

Stay alert to the all-too-human tendency to refuse to look at unpleasant realities. Make certain that the real failures of the old culture are exposed. Remind people frequently of the consequences of behaving in the old, dysfunctional ways.

STRATEGY 25: SACRIFICE THE SACRED COWS

Craft dramatic opportunities to separate people from the old ways and simultaneously create a strong emotional linkage to the new culture.

STRATEGY 26: TRANSFORM THE VOCABULARY

Make a list of terminology that reinforces the old culture and, through daily exercise, replace with a list of terminology that reinforces the new culture. Watch out for weasel-words, however—make sure that the new terminology actually reflects the new reality.

STRATEGY 27: REINFORCE THE NEW CULTURE

Make certain that every element of daily activity reinforces the new culture. Reward people for acting according to the new culture. Actively discourage actions that harken back to the bad old days.

STRATEGY 28: CREATE AN ELECTRONIC COMMUNITY

Use electronic mail to keep people in remote locations connected to the goals and social fabric of the corporate community.

STRATEGY 29: HANDLE E-MAIL WITH CARE

Be certain that your personal use of electronic mail doesn't create new communications problems in the organization.

STRATEGY 30: KEEP IT SHORT AND SIMPLE

Write like a journalist so that people can absorb and understand your ideas as quickly and easily as possible.

STRATEGY 31: RUTHLESSLY PRIORITIZE

Don't let the increased flow of information create a state of overflow. Understand where you're going and make certain that you're surrounded by information that helps you achieve that goal.

STRATEGY 32: CULTIVATE CONSTANT CHALLENGE

Avoid burnout by making certain that your job and the jobs of your employees are interesting and exciting.

STRATEGY 33: LEARN TO DISCONNECT

Find a physical or mental space where you can escape from the daily demands of the work environment. Learn to set complicated tasks aside when you need to rest.

STRATEGY 34: TAKE FREQUENT SABBATICALS

There will be times when you're going to have to work long hours. After doing so, take some time off to "recharge your batteries." There are also points in your career where a longer sabbatical can help you achieve the sense of balance that leads to lasting success.

Recommended Reading

The following is a list of publications that influenced me during the research and writing of this book. Some provided clarification of the ideas of the Electronic Elite; others provided the perspective of an opposing viewpoint. All are valuable for anyone interested in learning more about the Electronic Elite and the formation of corporate culture.

Scott Adams. *Build a Better Life by Stealing Office Supplies*. Kansas City: Andrews and McMeel. 1991. Through his simple drawings, Adams gives us ruthless snapshots of the Industrial Age business world as it really is. This book is particularly valuable because it punctures the self-important and pompous attitudes that make corporations so out of date. Each cartoon is a gem of wisdom.

Gil Amelio. *Profit from Experience: The National Semiconductor Story of Transformation Management*. New York: Van Nostrand Reinhold, 1996. An excellent and detailed example of how strong values and leadership can revolutionize a corporate culture.

Stanley Bing. *Crazy Bosses: Spotting Them, Serving Them, Surviving Them*. New York: Pocket Books. 1992. A descent into the Dante's inferno of paranoid and psychotic management. If this book doesn't convince you that something's fundamentally wrong with Industrial Age corporate culture, then nothing will. It contains examples of people who have actually been driven insane and suicidal by the organizations in which they work.

James Chposky and Ted Leonsis. *Blue Magic: The People, Power and Politics behind the IBM Personal Computer*. New York: Facts on File. 1988. A detailed description of how IBM's corporate culture destroyed the company's best chance for the future. Rather than treating the personal computer as an opportunity, IBM's old guard chained it up as if it were a Frankenstein monster. It's a textbook case of how Industrial Age management techniques are completely inadequate for fast-paced Information Age markets.

Robert X. Cringely. *Accidental Empires: How the Boys of Silicon Valley Make Their Millions, Battle Foreign Competition, and Still Can't Get a Date*. New York: Harper Business. 1992. An amusing if facile history of the computer industry, with an emphasis on the peculiarities, rather than the brilliances, of the Electronic Elite. The reader is left with the impression that a bunch of nerds accidentally made a lot of money, a vision of the computer industry that devalues the amazing contributions that the Electronic Elite have made to the evolution of the American corporation.

Terrence E. Deal and Allan A. Kennedy. *Corporate Cultures: The Rites and Rituals of Corporate Life*. Reading, MA: Addison-Wesley. 1982. One of the first books to treat corporate behavior as a cultural phenomenon. The authors build a powerful case for the influence of culture on behavior. Many of the companies profiled have Industrial Age cultures, and many, including IBM and Tandem, have suffered greatly since the book was published.

Bill Gates. *The Road Ahead*. New York: Viking, 1996. Bill describes his (and Microsoft's) vision for the future. While the book doesn't deal in detail with the cultural changes that the realization of Bill's vision will undoubtedly entail, it illustrates clearly that the pace of change is increasing, demanding a revision of our conceptual models for work and play.

Michael Hammer and James Champy. *Reengineering the Corporation: A Manifesto for Business Revolution*. New York: Harper Business. 1993. This much-discussed book prescribes massive changes in corporate processes and structure. The advice makes sense, but only if the cultures of the corporations that attempt reengineering are capable of absorbing and acting on the strategies that the authors suggest. The book does a good job of proving that reorganizations and other surface shufflings aren't going to make companies more competitive. It is most useful when combined with Champy's sequel, *Reengineering Management: The New Mandate for Leadership*, which deals with cultural change.

Dennis Hayes. *Behind the Silicon Curtain: The Seductions of Work in a Lonely Era*. Boston: South End Press. 1989. Hayes examines the lifestyles of the Electronic Elite and finds them lacking in depth. He focuses on some negative aspects of the computer industry and expands them into a central theme of misery and exploitation.

Guy Kawasaki. *Selling the Dream: How to Promote Your Product, Company, or Ideas—and Make a Difference—Using Everyday Evangelism*. New York: Harper Collins. 1991. Relentlessly upbeat, this book advances the conviction that product managers should literally act like religious fanatics when promoting their products. It is a particularly interesting read in light of the fact that Apple Computers—the apparent Mecca of product evangelism—has lost market share since the book was published.

Thomas Koulopoulos and Carl Frappaolo. *EDMS: A Portable Consultant*. New York: McGraw Hill, 1995. A refreshing and practical look at the intersection of technological change and business process reengineering. The case studies and analyses illustrate the critical importance of corporate culture on the management of both gradual and radical change.

Sandra L. Kurtzig (with Tom Parker). *CEO: Building a $400 Million Company from the Ground Up.* New York: W. W. Norton. 1991. The book describes, in interesting detail, how Kurtzig grew Ask Computer from a home business into a giant corporation. The book ends as she moves forward to repurchase Ask after leaving the company some years before. A good insider's view of the growth of a software company.

Stephen Manes and Paul Andrews. *Gates: How Microsoft's Mogul Reinvented an Industry—and Made Himself the Richest Man in America.* New York: Touchstone. 1994. An interesting study of the chairman of Microsoft, William H. Gates. The authors convey a great deal of the excitement about working in a high-tech company while lionizing the rise of Microsoft and Gates into almost mythical proportions. A fascinating read for anyone interested in the growth of the software market over the past 15 years.

Eric Nee, Editor-in-Chief. *Upside Magazine.* 2015 Pioneer Court, San Mateo, CA 94403. This award-winning magazine features interviews with computer industry leaders and highly insightful articles on technology, business, and the impact of both on society. It also features financial overviews of high-tech companies and columns by leading analysts. Anyone who's interested in an insider's perspective on the computer industry should subscribe.

David Packard. *The HP Way: How Bill Hewlett and I Built Our Company.* New York: Harper Business. 1995. This interesting book describes the whole story of how HP came to be the industry leader that it is today. The book contains numerous anecdotes that illustrate the evolution of a new form of management.

Tom Peters. *Liberation Management: Necessary Disorganization for the Nanosecond Nineties.* New York: Fawcett Columbine. 1992. In his quest to make a point about the disorganization of the modern world, Peters pushes the limit, forcing the reader to reevaluate ways of thinking about every aspect of business life.

Tom Peters. *Thriving on Chaos: Handbook for a Management Revolution.* New York: Harper Perennial. 1987. A massive, amazing tome that blasts nearly every aspect of the way that Industrial Age companies are managed, with numerous suggestions for quantum improvement. The reader is flooded with valuable ideas and practical approaches to implementing those ideas.

Glenn Rifkin and George Harrar. *The Ultimate Entrepreneur: The Story of Ken Olsen and Digital Equipment Corporation.* New York: Contemporary Books. 1988. Digital was flying high but running out of fuel when this classic investigation was written. The authors' analysis of the character of Digital founder Ken Olsen illustrates how the traits that make a great Industrial Age leader can be fatal in the Information Age.

242

Anthony Robbins. *Awaken the Giant Within: How to Take Immediate Control of Your Mental, Emotional, Physical and Financial Destiny.* New York: Fireside. 1991. This is primarily a book about personal development, but it also accurately describes (among many other things) the effect of belief upon behavior. Because cultures are made up of individuals, understanding the process by which an individual's beliefs create his or her destiny is tantamount to understanding how a culture's paradigms create its destiny.

Theodore Roszak. *The Cult of Information: The Folklore of Computers and the True Art of Thinking.* New York: Pantheon. 1986. Roszak mercilessly pokes holes in overbloated and overhyped computer "breakthroughs" such as artificial intelligence and the entire concept of "computer literacy." This book challenged everything that I once believed to be true about computer technology.

Michael Rothschild. *Bionomics: Economy as Ecosystem.* New York: John Macrae. 1990. An amazing book that represents the first major rethinking of economic theory in the past 100 years. Rothschild transcends the writings of traditional economists by pointing out the close parallels of economic and biological evolution. A seminal work that's influencing an entire generation of thinkers in many different fields, the book is also popular among the Electronic Elite.

Anne Wilson Schaef and Diane Fassel. *The Addictive Organization.* New York: Harper and Row. 1988. This book takes the popular notion of addiction and maps it onto the habitual behaviors that take place inside organizations. The book then prescribes a recovery method that's based upon the 12-step program of Alcoholics Anonymous.

Alvin Toffler. *The Third Wave.* New York: William Morrow. 1980. The best way to evaluate futurists and fortunetellers is with 20/20 hindsight. Toffler's work has proven uncanny in its predictions of the social effect of our increasingly computerized world.

Shoshana Zuboff. *In the Age of the Smart Machine: The Future of Work and Power.* New York: Basic Books. 1988. A fascinating study of the effect of computerization at several corporations. Zuboff looks at how the workplace and employees have had to change to accommodate computer technology. Her work amply illustrates the toxic nature of the combination of Industrial Age management and Information Age technology.

Index